Changing Cultures in Congress

WOODROW WILSON CENTER SERIES

WOODROW WILSON CENTER SERIES

The Woodrow Wilson International Center for Scholars was chartered by the U.S. Congress in 1968 as the living memorial to the nation's twenty-eighth president. It serves as the country's key nonpartisan policy forum, tackling global challenges through independent research and open dialogue. Bridging the worlds of academia and public policy, the Center's diverse programmatic activity informs actionable ideas for Congress, the administration, and the broader policy community.

The Woodrow Wilson Center Series shares in the Center's mission by publishing outstanding scholarly and public-policy-related books for a global readership. Written by the Center's expert staff and international network of scholars, our books shed light on a wide range of topics, including U.S. foreign and domestic policy, security, the environment, energy, and area studies.

Conclusions or opinions expressed in Center publications and programs are those of the authors and speakers and do not necessarily reflect the views of the Center staff, fellows, trustees, advisory groups, or any individuals or organizations that provide financial support for the Center.

Please visit us online at www.wilsoncenter.org.

Changing Cultures in Congress

From Fair Play to Power Plays

Donald R. Wolfensberger

COLUMBIA UNIVERSITY PRESS

NEW YORK

Columbia University Press
Publishers Since 1893
New York   Chichester, West Sussex
cup.columbia.edu
Copyright © 2018 Columbia University Press
All rights reserved

Library of Congress Cataloging-in-Publication Data

Names: Wolfensberger, Donald R., author.
Title: Changing cultures in Congress : from fair play to power plays /
Donald R. Wolfensberger.
Description: New York : Columbia University Press, 2018. | Series: Woodrow Wilson
Center series | Includes bibliographical references and index.
Identifiers: LCCN 2018015837 | ISBN 9780231190145 (cloth : alk. paper) |
ISBN 9780231190152 (pbk. : alk. paper) | ISBN 9780231548748 (e-book)
Subjects: LCSH: United States. Congress. House—Rules and practice. | United States.
Congress. House—Elections. | Parliamentary practice—United States.
Classification: LCC KF4992 .W65 2018 | DDC 328.73—dc23
LC record available at https://lccn.loc.gov/2018015837

Columbia University Press books are printed on permanent
and durable acid-free paper.
Printed in the United States of America

Cover design: Noah Arlow

Contents

Contents

Acknowledgments

FIRST AND FOREMOST, I want to thank my wife, Monty Tripp, for patiently, painstakingly, and prudently editing this book. Not only is she scrupulous in correcting my sometimes awkward sentences but, as with my previous book, she is full of good ideas on what things should be included in (or excluded from) a chapter—even occasionally recommending a different chapter in place of one that lacked pizzazz.

Second, I want to thank the two institutions that have housed me over the past several years as a fellow. The Woodrow Wilson International Center for Scholars has been my work home since I retired from Congress in 1997. It enabled me to write my first book when I arrived, and then to run the Congress Project from 1999 to 2012.

We have been fortunate to have two former members of Congress—Lee Hamilton and Jane Harman—as presidents of the Wilson Center since 1999. Their leadership, both in the House of Representatives and then at the Wilson Center, has been an inspiration to our scholars and staff alike.

Joe Brinley, former director of the Woodrow Wilson Center Press, was responsible for doggedly urging me to write a second book. He had conscientiously overseen the production of my first book, *Congress and the People: Deliberative Democracy on Trial*. Although he retired before seeing this book completed, I hope he will not be disappointed in the fulfillment of his entreaties.

I am deeply indebted to Alfred F. Imhoff, a long-standing editor of Wilson Center books, for his meticulous flyspecking of my manuscript, his patient understanding of the many changes I made along the way, and for his constructive suggestions. Columbia University Press editor Stephen Wesley was likewise a very helpful and encouraging partner in this enterprise, as were Robert Litwak and Suzanne Napper at the Wilson Center in overseeing the book's completion. I extend kudos to Wilson Center librarian Janet Spikes and her staff for their prompt and efficient help in retrieving books from the Library of Congress and in conducting both online and hard-copy searches in the center's marvelous reference library.

I am also grateful to Jason Grumet, president of the Bipartisan Policy Center (BPC), for offering me a fellowship in 2011 at the urging of John Fortier, director of the Democracy Project. This dual affiliation immediately led to a series of six roundtable discussions on the topic "The Culture of Congress" that were cosponsored by and alternated between the Wilson Center and BPC. And these discussions led me to write a summary report, "Getting Back to Legislating," which served as background material for BPC's Commission on Political Reform in 2013–14.

I was honored to serve as a resource person on congressional reform for this commission as it carried out its deliberations in Washington and around the country. This experience prompted me to rethink many of the ideas I had formed while in Congress that had been reflected in my first book. It forced me to reconsider Congress from new angles and ensured that this book would not simply be a rewrite of my first one. John Fortier's deputy at

BPC, Matt Weil, and BPC senior policy analyst Michael Thorning have also been important influences in our ongoing conversations about Congress, politics, and governing.

Finally, I want to thank colleagues both in the political science profession and in Congress (members and staff alike) who are too numerous to name here, for their friendship, counsel, and participation in our programs at BPC and the Wilson Center over the years. You have proven Woodrow Wilson so right when he observed that the scholar and policymaker both benefit from a mutual exchange of ideas.

I dedicate this book to all my fellow institutionalists whom I have had the privilege to know and work with for more than four decades in this town. Your faith and dedication to our representative democracy have reinforced and fueled my own work and commitment to strengthening the bonds between the people and their elected representatives. It is not a lonely nor lost cause—it is a just cause. And just causes have a way of eventually prevailing.

Changing Cultures in Congress

Introduction

SHORTLY AFTER THE REPUBLICANS took control of Congress in 1995, the House Rules Committee vice chairman, Republican representative David Dreier of California, formed a task force on committee reform. His goal was to keep alive the drive among junior members of Congress to pursue further institutional changes beyond those put in place on the opening day of the new, 104th Congress. The new majority, for instance, had backed off making significant changes in committee jurisdictions to avoid starting a turf war between newly anointed committee chairpersons.

Made up primarily of reform-minded members of the GOP freshman class, the group met privately early in the first session with a handful of sympathetic supporters from academia and think tanks. Dreier asked the guests what surprised them most about the new Republican majority. Without hesitating, one of the guests sadly replied, "I didn't think you would become them so soon." Several of the members and guests nodded in silent agreement. No further explanation was necessary. Everyone knew that the reference was to the previous Democratic majority in the House and its high-handed ways of running the institution. What was startling was that the newly emergent majority was already being flagged for engaging in the same kind of arrogant power plays they had charged the old Democratic majority with pursuing during its forty-year-long control of the House of Representatives.

As the Rules Committee's Republican staff director, I was monitoring the session for my chairman, Republican representative Jerry Solomon of New York. As the ranking minority member on the Rules Committee in the previous Congress, Solomon had been a pit bull, going after the Democratic majority for its abusive tactics. He decried taking procedural shortcuts, usually at the expense of the defenseless minority party. Solomon and Dreier had taken the lead in making sure that the Contract with America, on which House Republicans ran in 1994, was unequivocal about the different ways in which a GOP majority would operate the institution—more openness, fairness, transparency, and accountability to the American people. The contract's reformist thrust was captured in such phrases as "to restore the bonds of trust between the people and their elected representatives," "to restore accountability to Congress," and "to make us all proud again of the way free people govern themselves."

Solomon even went further than the contract in pledging to reverse the trend toward fewer amendments on major legislation from 70 percent restrictive rules to 70 percent open rules. His heart was in the right place, but the final tally for the 104th Congress was only 58 percent open rules. In fact, the new Republican leadership began the opening day of the session by scheduling a major congressional reform bill under a closed rule, setting a bad example from the outset. It proceeded to employ many of the other procedural shortcuts the previous majority had favored, including the self-executing adoption of amendments, consideration of unreported bills, omnibus bills rushed through without adequate time to digest their contents, and on and on. Although the overall record of House Republicans in the 104th Congress offered at least some improvement over the previous Congress under the Democrats, they could not boast the dramatic turnaround in congressional operations promised in their campaign platform.

I retired in early 1997 and came to the Woodrow Wilson International Center for Scholars. In 1999, I joined the staff of the center as director of the Congress Project. My aim was to better educate the public about how Congress worked, using various policy issues as a template against which to examine the politics, processes, and personalities that drive policymaking on Capitol Hill.

By the time my book, *Congress and the People: Deliberative Democracy on Trial*, neared completion in early 1999, the experience of the 105th Congress had convinced me that the directions charted in the 104th Congress were not an aberration. Republicans continued to expand their procedural abuses and shortcuts. One chapter, "Coming Full Circle: The Complete Revolution?," foreshadowed the title I had originally intended for this book: *The Animal Farm Congress: How Political Revolutions Come Full Circle.* By then I had the benefit not only of reflecting on what I had participated in but also of viewing subsequent developments from a five-year remove.

Moreover, I benefited from reading Newt Gingrich's 1998 reflections on his first term as speaker of the House. In *Lessons Learned the Hard Way*, Gingrich wrote that the pressures of rounding up sufficient votes were so great that the Republican majority was pushed into the mode of inducing conformity: "Thus there is a permanent danger that like the animals in George Orwell's *Animal Farm*, we might gradually come to resemble the very machine we had replaced." But he quickly added that Republicans would never become as bad as the Democrats had been because the GOP was the party of ideas, and it was in its best interest to promote open debate, dissent, and argument.[1]

Nevertheless, shortly after publication of Gingrich's book, journalist Ron Elving reported on how the Republicans were handling legislation in the House, drawing on the same analogy used by the speaker: "Like the elevated animals that overthrew the farmer in George Orwell's 'Animal Farm,' they have learned how the experience of power transforms 'four legs good, two legs bad' into 'four legs good, two legs better.'" Republicans had begun imitating the ways of their former masters, Elving observed, and despite their earlier critique of the Democrats' management, "the demands of regime have taken precedence over the idea of reform. So it is that revolutions age."[2]

This pattern persisted throughout the reign of Republicans in the House from 1995 to 2006. In their 2006 campaign platform, "A New Direction for America," the House Democrats made a "promise to the American people" in their "Honest Leadership and Open Government" plank to restore the regular order to legislative proceedings. That would include "open, full, and fair debate," with "a full amendment process that grants the Minority the right to offer its alternatives." Yet, with hardly a pause, the Democrats slipped into the old ways of doing things at the very outset of the 110th Congress.

When the Republicans regained control of the House with the 2010 elections, there was a brief breath of fresh air with the ascension to the speakership of Representative John Boehner (R-OH), a former committee chairman and legislator, who promised that this time the Republicans were serious about restoring the regular order to the House by giving committees and the minority party a fuller role in the legislative process. Despite improvements at the outset, the data on procedural abuses and restrictive practices did not vary much (see the appendix). Republicans were still not able to return the institution to the deliberative lawmaking body both parties had claimed they wanted while in the minority.

Ironically, the decisive revolt against the majority Republican leadership's tightening grip on the process came not from minority Democrats but from a small group of Tea Party Republicans in the House. In April 2015, one of the Freedom Caucus members, Representative Mark Meadows of North Carolina, introduced a resolution "declaring the office of the Speaker of the House of Representatives vacant"—a roundabout way of saying Speaker John Boehner was dethroned. The resolution even included a bill of particulars in its preamble, or so-called whereas clauses. These included complaints of top-down management of the House by the speaker while bypassing members, punishing members who vote contrary to the speaker's wishes, and limiting the ability of members to amend bills because of the speaker's control over the Rules Committee.[3]

The resolution's eight-part preamble destroyed the privilege of the resolution, meaning it could not be immediately called up on the House floor, but it did have the effect of igniting an internal debate among GOP conference members, which led the speaker to announce in late September that he would step down at the end of October, or when his successor was chosen.

This successor, Representative Paul Ryan of Wisconsin, was sworn in on October 29, 2015. He conceded in his acceptance speech that "the House is broken" and that "neither members nor the people are satisfied with how things are going," and he pledged to change the way the House does business by letting committees take the lead in drafting legislation and letting members, including the minority, contribute and participate in the process through debate and amendments. In short, Ryan was promising what his predecessors had promised over the previous two decades. In his words, "We need to return to the regular order."[4]

The recurring pattern of political revolutions coming full circle, with the insurgents eventually copying the ways of their former masters, is what prompted my original interest in calling this book *The Animal Farm Congress*. I subsequently opted for a different title, *Changing Cultures in Congress: From Fair Play to Power Plays*, because it goes deeper into the motivations and methods that power the modern-day Congress. It implies a win-at-all-costs mentality that throws caution, fairness, and deliberative policy-making to the winds. This phenomenon must be better understood if we ever hope to reverse what I have previously termed "the culture of the perpetual campaign."

In witnessing the three congressional revolts since 1994—both between and within parties in 2006, 2010, and 2015—I realized I had to do a better job of figuring out why it happens and whether it is forever bound to repeat itself. In answering these questions, I needed to more clearly understand what the founders intended for the institution as it developed, and why it has strayed from that vision in modern times as Congress has been wracked by high partisanship and turmoil.

It is the thesis of this book that Congress has evolved over the decades from a culture of legislating to a culture of campaigning at the expense of serious deliberation to solve major problems confronting the nation. This trend has accelerated and been exacerbated since the Republican takeover of the House in 1995, but its roots were sown in the 1970s with the congressional reform revolution that dethroned powerful committee chairpersons and replaced their rule by the new reign of party leaders accountable to the majority party caucus.

Although this fulfilled the dream of some political scientists and progressive politicians to usher in a new system of "responsible party government," it also began chipping away at open committee deliberations to devise broadly acceptable solutions. The initial breakdown in the old ways in favor of a more free-wheeling majority party soon yielded to the development and adoption of the legislative agenda by party leaders, increasingly by stretching and bending long-standing rules of fairness or orderly legislating.

To protect party legislation, the majority leadership has used the House Rules Committee to produce restrictive amendment rules and other procedural gimmicks for the floor consideration of bills, usually to the detriment of minority party participation. But this process depends on majority party members' acquiescence in the truncated process and procedures, pushing all but key committee chairpersons out of significant roles in policymaking.

With party leaders doing the heavy legislative lifting, rank-and-file members not only lose interest in legislating but also in conducting meaningful oversight of government agencies and programs—the fundamental predicate to sound policymaking. By 2018, members of both parties were expressing widespread dissatisfaction with Congress and its inability to get even its basic budgeting work done, let alone address growing national problems.[5]

This book provides a historical perspective on the evolving process and procedures of Congress, with primary emphasis on the House of Representatives, and explores through case studies how partisan majorities devise and exploit new rules and procedures for maximum legislative and electoral success in areas such as health care, budgeting, and foreign policy. Finally, I suggest ways to put Congress back on a course to deliberative lawmaking in the national interest.

Some of the procedural maneuvers described in this book may be baffling to the lay reader. To assist the reader, a glossary at the end of the book defines some of the arcane terms found throughout the text.

1

Rolling Rules

From Level Ground to Partisan Tilt

THE FOUNDERS OF THE republic knew that a fair and inclusive process was essential to the proper functioning of the fragile new government. Competing factions, operating under just rules, could come together to forge consensus policies. However, a century later, Congress was hopelessly gridlocked over too much legislation and obstructive minority tactics. Consequently, innovative new procedures were introduced and implemented through the Rules Committee of the House of Representatives, under strong speakers, to ensure that a House majority could work its will. However, it could no longer be said that the rules were completely fair to minorities. The modern-day House that gradually emerged replaced fair play with power plays.

In his *Manual of Parliamentary Practice for the Use of the Senate of the United States*, Thomas Jefferson stresses the importance of having a body of rules to guide a parliamentary body: "It is much more material that there should be a rule to go by than what that rule is," he wrote, "that there may be a uniformity of proceeding in business not subject to the caprice of the Speaker, or captiousness of the members." Only by adopting and adhering to such a uniform set of rules of proceeding, Jefferson continued, can "order, decency, and regularity be preserved in a dignified public body."[1]

A century later, in an essay published just a few months before he was to be sworn in as speaker of the House for the first time, Representative Thomas Brackett Reed cast a totally different light on the role of rules: "If the majority do not govern, the minority will; and if the tyranny of the majority is hard, the tyranny of the minority is simply unendurable. The rules, then, ought to be so arranged as to facilitate the actions of the majority."[2]

Reed would turn Jefferson's *Manual* on its head by asserting the prerogative of speakers of the House to issue rulings from the chair to enforce majority rule over minority rights and obstructionism, and then use the House Rules Committee, which the speaker chaired, to incorporate those rulings into the standing rules of the House. This chapter briefly explores how and why the House quickly evolved from being governed by a neutral set of rules to a system under which the majority would dominate the institution through rules dictated at the caprice of speakers and backed by the captiousness of partisan majorities.

In the Beginning

The framers of the Constitution well understood the importance of rules in a parliamentary body. It took them just nine words to bestow on Congress this fundamental rulemaking responsibility: "Each House may determine the rules of its proceedings."[3] One need look no further than the writings of the father of the Constitution, James Madison, in *The Federalist Papers* to understand just how important the founders considered that rulemaking responsibility as a defense against arbitrary power being exercised at the expense of minorities. In *Federalist* No. 10, Madison opens by alluding to concerns that Congress might end up on the same bad path as some state governments: "Complaints are everywhere heard . . . that our governments are unstable; that the public good is disregarded in the conflicts of rival parties; and that measures are too often decided, not according to the rules of justice, and the rights of the minor party, but by the superior force of an interested and overbearing majority."[4]

As political scientist Greg Weiner has pointed out, what Madison meant by "justice" in that passage "was a procedural standard guaranteeing that decisions would be made according to known rules." Madison was not arguing against majority rule, says Weiner, but rather against the arbitrary and unpredictable rule of majorities "on the basis of sheer force." Throughout Madison's writings, according to Weiner, "justice is generally associated with fairness and rules rather than substance and political decisions." The important thing was that majorities reached their decisions in a fair rather than arbitrary manner to ensure "a stable and predictable environment."[5]

It is within this procedural context that Madison goes on to explain in *Federalist* No. 10 that the central role of Congress is "to refine and enlarge the public views by passing them through the medium of a chosen body of citizens whose wisdom may best discern the true interest of their country and whose patriotism and love of justice will be least likely to sacrifice it to temporary or partial considerations." For such deliberation to take place, rules and procedures are required that allow all members to participate in the process. This is the best safeguard against a majority faction invading the rights of other citizens.

Madison understood that factions were an inevitable part of any free society and therefore saw "the principal task of modern legislation" as being "the regulation of these various and interfering interests" by involving "the spirit of party and faction in the necessary and ordinary operations of government." Put another way, the dangers of factions are best mitigated by ensuring that all factions are fully and fairly represented in the regular decision-making processes of Congress. For this to succeed, a set of rules is required that is impartial and does not allow a single party or faction to dominate either the rulemaking or legislative processes.[6]

A decade after Hamilton, Madison, and Jay wrote and published their *Federalist* essays in support of the Constitution, Thomas Jefferson set about compiling his *Manual of Parliamentary Practice* in his role as presiding officer of the Senate while serving as vice president from 1797 to 1800. In the preface to his *Manual*, Jefferson expresses the hope that future generations will build on his work "till a code of rules shall be formed . . . the effects of which may be accuracy in business, economy of time, order, uniformity, and impartiality."[7]

It is from Jefferson and his *Manual* that we get not only one of the best explanations of the necessity of a "code of rules" but also the fullest attempt up to that point to provide a detailed, operating guide for organizing a legislature and processing its business. In his opening, Jefferson cites former British House of Commons speaker Arthur Onslow's reference to an oft-repeated maxim passed on to him as a young man by the older, more experienced members of Parliament: Nothing throws power into the hands of administration more "than a neglect of, or departure from the rules of proceeding," which are "a shelter and protection to the minority against the attempts at power."[8]

When the First Congress convened in Philadelphia in March 1789, most members were already familiar with basic legislative procedures, having previously served in the Continental Congress, their state legislatures, and some at the Constitutional Convention. The rules of these earlier American legislative bodies were essentially derived from English parliamentary practices and precedents on which Jefferson would also draw (only in much deeper detail than the average member of Congress could begin to appreciate). It is therefore not surprising that both houses of the new Congress adopted similar sets of rules with relative ease in

April 1789, shortly after mustering quorums in New York City's Federal Hall.

On April 2, the House created an eleven-member Select Committee on Rules "to prepare and report such standing rules and orders of proceeding as may be proper to be observed in the House." The select committee chose Representative Elias Boudinot of New Jersey as its chairman. Boudinot, who previously served one term as president of the Continental Congress, is described by former representative De Alva Stanwood Alexander in his history of the House as "a far-seeing, benevolent dictator whose patriotic words acted as a tonic."[9] Other members of the Rules Committee included the oldest member of the First Congress, Representative Roger Sherman of Connecticut. James Madison was also a member of the committee, there to help ensure his design of government would work.[10]

The first set of twelve rules spelled out the following: (1) the duties of the speaker to preside over the House, preserve order and decorum, decide points of order, announce results of votes, and appoint committees of three or fewer members (the House soon extended that authority to all committees rather than require the election of committee members); (2) the rules of decorum and debate; (3) procedures for the introduction and disposition of bills; (4) the right of members to speak no more than twice on the same subject (later changed to once per subject); (5) the operation of committees of the whole House; and (6) the use of motions for the previous question, to amend, commit, or adjourn.[11]

Fewer than two months after the House adopted its first set of rules, Madison complained in a letter to his friend, Edmund Randolph, that "in every step, the difficulties arising from the novelty are severely experienced," and that "scarcely a day passes without some striking evidence of the delays and perplexities springing merely from the want of precedents." He optimistically added that "time will be a full remedy for this evil; and will, I am persuaded, evince a greater facility in legislating uniformly for all the states."[12] Nevertheless, the worry was already there that without a uniform set of precedents behind the rules the legislative path would be a rocky one—something Jefferson would at least attempt to partially remedy through the publication of his *Manual*.

A Partisan Rules Theory

It is not accurate to argue, as some do, that the flaw in the framers' design was that it did not contemplate the emergence of political parties and how they might upset the delicate, constitutional balances created. Madison, in *Federalist* No. 10, warned about the dangers of factions; and parties are, after all, simply an agglomeration of factions or interest groups. Moreover, Madison called attention to the negative impacts "rival parties" were already having in some states by running roughshod over minority rights through their use of "superior force" as opposed to a reliance on "the rules of justice." Just as Madison acknowledged that factions are inevitable in a free republic—"Liberty is to faction what air is to fire"—he was well aware that parties, or megafactions, were more than inevitable: they could endanger the survival of the republic.

Indeed, the spirit of party was already evident at the time federalists Madison, Jay, and Hamilton were arguing for ratification of the Constitution in dueling essays with their antifederalist opponents. Although those two forces did not formally organize as political parties in the First Congress, the debates on many issues, including over how extensive a Bill of Rights should be, clearly broke down along those same lines.[13] The partisan lines of demarcation began to harden and take shape after George Washington's two unopposed terms as president, when the Jeffersonian Republicans emerged to take on the Hamilton-Adams Federalists in the elections of 1796 and 1800.

Nonetheless, the system of neutral rules in both houses of Congress held beyond those divisive elections as Congress continued to grow, evolve, and adapt to changing circumstances. Many historians and political scientists argue that the real partisan takeover of the House and its rules occurred during the speakership of Republican representative Thomas Brackett Reed in the late 1800s. That view is largely correct given Reed's enormously successful efforts to finally break up minority party obstructionism and enable a House majority to work its will on legislation of its choosing. However, political scientist Sarah Binder argues that partisan manipulation of the institution's rules began long before that. In *Minority Rights, Majority Rule*, she puts forth a "theory of the partisan basis of procedural choice" that traces the emergence of party-driven rules to disputes over the previous question motion in the House during the run-up to the war of 1812.[14]

The 1789 House rule on what the previous question motion meant was posed as follows: "Shall the main question be now put?" However, as Alexander points out in his history of the House, in the House of Commons and in the Congress of the Confederation the rule was worded in the form of a negative: "Shall the main question be *not* now put?" In that instance, if the previous question motion was adopted, debate would continue. It was Rules Committee chairman Boudinot who successfully recommended to his committee that the "not" be dropped: if the previous question motion was adopted, debate on the main question ceased; whereas if the question motion was rejected, debate went over to the next day. Under that first House rule for the previous question, the motion could only be admitted on the demand of five members, and, "until it is decided," the demand "shall preclude all amendment and further debate of the main question." However, each member could still speak, not more than once, on the merits of the motion.[15]

Throughout the first century of Congress, arguments and rulings went back and forth in the House on whether all debate must end when the previous question is moved. The House in 1805 presumably eliminated the right to first debate the previous question motion before voting on it. But the tug-of-war over interpretations and enforcement continued, not so much between parties as among individuals who did not relish giving up any of their rights to speak freely and for as long as they wished.

Binder makes a critical point in noting that the issue came to a head in a partisan way in 1811 through the "War Hawks," led by Henry Clay. At the time of the clash in the House, Clay was still in the Senate, cheering on his feathered brethren. But he would join them in the next Congress as a House member and immediately be elected speaker. The hawkish majority essentially imposed its will and interpretation of the previous question motion to stifle antiwar filibusters and to bring their war-preparedness bills to a vote (birds of a feather, war together). Under their new (or original) interpretation, the demand for the previous question would immediately be voted on, without further debate, and, if adopted, the pending measure would be brought to a final vote.[16]

Consequently, the first war-preparedness bill passed, as would others, perhaps ironically, in aid of the administration of President James Madison, that staunch proponent of "the rules of justice." However, after that partisan, wartime push for strict enforcement of the previous question, the motion fell into disuse for at least two decades and, writes Alexander, "the House dropped back into the vice of unlimited debate."[17]

Binder makes a convincing case, building on the previous question case study, that procedural changes in the House are driven primarily by partisan considerations and strength. Majority parties are more likely to change rules in their favor if they believe such changes will enhance their chances of legislative success, especially when minority party obstructionism hampers the majority's legislative goals. Conversely, when majority parties are weak and cross-party coalitions emerge, minority rights are expanded, at least until majorities grow strong again and can take back those rights—like selfish children reclaiming their toys in the sandbox.[18]

Despite sporadic attempts to limit debate throughout the nineteenth century, Alexander notes in his history that the century was characterized by "constant warfare" over minority obstructionism that "resulted in limiting the rights of the minority and entrenching the power of the majority."[19]

By 1880, the House was tied in knots and took bold action to revise its rules. A select committee on rules proposed paring the mishmash of 166 rules down to a package of just 44 rules, the principal aims of which were, in an intentional bow to Jefferson's *Manual*, "to secure accuracy in business, economy of time, order, uniformity and impartiality and to prepare if possible a simple, concise and non-partisan code of rules." The select committee was careful to assert it was not out to upset the balance between majority rule and minority rights. Rather, its goal was to guarantee both the right of the majority "to control and dispose of the business for which it is held responsible" and not to invade or restrict "the powers of a minority to check, temporarily, if not permanently, the action of a majority believed to be improper or unconstitutional."[20]

Among other things, the new rules established legislative calendars to ensure greater efficiency, enumerated the jurisdiction of the forty-eight standing committees, and made the Rules Committee a permanent standing committee with jurisdiction over "all proposed action touching on rules and joint rules." However, as Alexander notes, "by shunning 'riders' and the 'disappearing quorum,' they left the real red-light district undisturbed."[21] These latter challenges would be taken up by Thomas Brackett Reed of Maine using the newly created standing Committee on Rules as his base, even before he became speaker and its chairman nine years later.

Reed's Campaign for Majority Rule

Although only in his third term as a House member, Reed was appointed to the new standing Committee on Rules in January 1882 as one of its three majority members. He quickly saw the potential for the new committee and its powers to report at any time on changes in House rules. His goals were to give priority floor consideration to legislation favored by the majority leadership and to eliminate obstructive and dilatory motions. He moved quickly to present reports from the Rules Committee to implement both of these goals through rules changes.

The first proposed rule would allow the House, by majority vote, to permit the immediate consideration of a bill, no matter what its position on the calendar, rather than requiring either unanimous consent or mustering a two-thirds vote to suspend the rules to do so. The effort failed when a majority quorum could not be obtained to consider the matter.

Reed waited until late May 1882 and a disputed election case to spring the second rule change: outlawing dilatory tactics. When the Democrats attempted to block action on the rule change with a motion to adjourn, Reed raised a point of order that such a motion was dilatory because it would prevent the House from addressing one of its most basic constitutional duties—judging election returns. The speaker upheld the point of order, and the rule change was adopted as it applies to election cases. As the House Rules Committee history notes, all this presaged the modern speakership and the House that Reed would build when he ascended to that office.[22]

Reed would get another run at his majority vote idea for considering bills out of order. As the 47th Congress drew to a close in early 1883, and with it the Republican majority reign in the House, Reed engineered a special rule change to enable a simple majority to vote to suspend the rules and send to a House-Senate conference a tariff bill stalled at the speaker's table.

The rule was so controversial that Reed lost thirty-two of his own party members to the Democrats' disappearing quorum (by refusing to answer when their names were called). However, the following day enough members recorded their presence for quorum purposes to adopt the rule and send the bill to conference. The measure was signed into law by Republican president Chester A. Arthur on March 3 as the 47th Congress expired.[23] This was only the second time in which a special rule (which would also come to be known as *special orders* or *order of business resolutions*) was devised to facilitate the disposition of a specific piece of legislation by majority vote on the rule.[24]

The advantage of special rules, which are simple House resolutions, is that they allow measures to be taken up immediately and out of the order on which they are placed on the calendar, and they also permit limits on general debate time and on what amendments can be offered to a bill. The device was perfected over the following decades and today remains the central focus of Rules Committee meetings to clear the way for floor consideration of major legislation on the majority's agenda.

Reed's Speakership

Republicans returned to power in 1889 after four years in the minority and elected Reed as their speaker. Reed previously was his party's de facto leader while in the minority. Now, as chairman of the Rules Committee, he purposely did not convene it to report rules for the new Congress. Instead, he proceeded to execute his carefully crafted plan to make major changes in House rules.

With the House still operating under general parliamentary law, Reed launched his initial offensive in a series of rulings he propounded from the chair from January 29 through 31, 1890. The rulings outlawed various minority tactics that had long been employed to slow down or block majority party legislative priorities. His rulings produced pandemonium in the House Chamber as angry Democrats erupted in a storm of protests—charging the podium waving clenched fists, shouting points of order and epithets of "tyrant" and "czar."

The matter under debate was a resolution declaring the Republican candidate the winner in a contested West Virginia election case. Democrats attempted to block debate on the resolution by employing the tactic of a disappearing quorum. Reed responded by directing the clerk to take down the names of members he reported as being present. One Democrat, Representative James McCreary, angrily protested, "I deny your right, Mr. Speaker, to count me as present." Reed calmly responded: "The Chair is making a statement of fact that the gentleman from Kentucky is present. Does he deny it? [*Laughter and applause on the Republican side.*]"[25]

When the disappearing quorum ploy failed, Democrats resorted to calling for repetitive votes on adjournment motions and appeals from rulings of the chair to further stall proceedings. But Reed blocked their moves by refusing to entertain what he called "dilatory motions."

In explaining the rationale for his quorum counting and dilatory motions rulings, Reed went to the heart of what he thought parliamentary bodies should be all about: "There is no possible way which the orderly methods of parliamentary procedures can be used to stop legislation. The object of a parliamentary body is action, and not the stoppage of action." If any member or group of members attempt to oppose the orderly progress of business, he continued, even using recognized parliamentary motions, "it is the right of the majority to refuse to have those motions entertained and to cause the public business to proceed."[26]

Reed then proceeded to the House Rules Committee, which he chaired, to incorporate his rulings, along with other changes he had in mind, into the standing rules of the House. All told, forty-five changes were made in House rules as reported by Reed's Rules Committee and then adopted on a party-line vote by the House. In addition to the quorum and dilatory motion rules, the new code reduced the quorum requirement in the Committee of the Whole from a majority to one hundred members provided that a majority of that quorum could close debate on any portion of the bill, and provided for the rapid processing of matters at the speaker's table, including the speaker's authority to refer bills to their respective committees without debate.[27]

Although Reed's Rules Committee would not bar all amendments using special rules, as is frequently done today, it would set dates and a time certain for a final vote on a bill. This was done, for instance, on the McKinley tariff and federal election (civil rights) measures in 1890. Moreover, the special rule on a silver purchase bill barred all substitute amendments.[28]

Speaker Reed's legislative successes in the historic 51st Congress, made possible by procedural innovations, did not protect his majority in the following election. In 1890, House Republicans took a drubbing at the polls, dropping from a 173 majority party, to an 88-member minority, with Democrats controlling 231 seats. Price increases from the McKinley tariff act kicked in just before the election and were largely credited with the losses. "Every woman who went to a store and tried to buy [something] went home to complain, and a wild unrest filled the public mind." Reed observed, "The wonder is that we got any votes at all."[29]

Majority Democrats, under Speaker Charles Crisp of Georgia, initially jettisoned the Reed rules in the 51st Congress. However, by the following Congress, after their own frustrating experiences with disappearing Republican quorums, they embraced a modified version of Reed's quorum counting rule. Moreover, under Crisp's chairmanship, the role of the Rules Committee in reporting special rules for considering legislation was further strengthened. By 1895, Republicans were back in control of the House and Reed was back as speaker and Rules Committee chairman.

Reed's Legacy

Most political science and history texts credit "the Reed Rules" as the speaker's greatest legacy. These rules did indeed usher in the modern Congress and more efficient ways of doing business by eradicating excessive minority obstruction. However, it was Reed's frequent use of special rules, and their institutionalization by the House, that became his most significant contribution as speaker—although, at times, when carried to their logical extremes, they were a troubling and controversial device.

The Reed Rules became embedded in the standing rules of the House and were, therefore, accepted as the normal order of business. However, as Onslow's maxim states, special rules were, by their very nature, "a neglect of, or departure from, the rules of proceeding" and could "throw power into the hands of administration." Or, to quote Jefferson, special rules could expose the House to "the caprice of the speaker or captiousness of members," thereby stripping minorities of their only "shelter and protection" against the attempts at power.[30]

Another legacy left by Reed that is not recognized widely is his shift in control of the rulemaking power at the beginning of a Congress. Previously, the new rules were reported to the House by the Rules Committee and considered under an open floor debate and amendment process. Reed changed that to put the majority party caucus in control, with its recommended rules considered under very limited debate and no amendments. He implanted this new system when he regained the speakership in 1895. He had the resolution adopting House rules considered at the beginning of that Congress as privileged from the floor, even though the Rules Committee had not yet been appointed. Moreover, the resolution was considered under the hour rule, without opportunity for amendment unless the minority managed to defeat the previous question—an exercise in futility because members are drilled by their elders on opening day to stick with the party in their votes on its nominee for speaker and adoption of the party-blessed House rules package.

That practice evolved until today the standard practice is to recognize the majority leader (or the presumptive Rules Committee chairman) to call up the resolution adopting House rules for the new Congress "by direction of" the Republican Conference (or, in the case of the Democrats in recent times, simply as a "privileged resolution" that did not even have prior caucus approval). As a matter of courtesy, the majority yields the minority one-half of the allotted hour "for the purposes of debate only," but not for amendment—the same procedure is used today for considering special rule resolutions from the Rules Committee providing for consideration of legislation.

Reed's final legacy ensured that the majority party would retain total control of all House rulemaking—from the adoption of House standing rules on opening day of a new Congress through the adoption of special rules each week for the consideration of major legislation.[31] The next chapter explains how these two rulemaking powers, both standing and special, have even been combined on the opening day of a new Congress to advance the majority's legislative agenda.

2

Making House Rules

SPEAKER THOMAS BRACKETT REED set the table for succeeding Congresses to adopt the partisan majority's set of House rules at the beginning of each Congress. The process theoretically takes only an hour, but in recent times the minority has exercised more procedural options in attempts to substitute its own rules package. Even when new majorities take charge, with promises of a fairer and more open system, they immediately revert to power plays—not only to adopt their set of House rules but even to pass legislation.

This chapter begins with the high drama of Nancy Pelosi's first day as Democratic speaker of the House in 2007. The chapter concludes with a look back at the revolt against Republican speaker Joe Cannon of Illinois in 1910 that removed him as chairman of the Rules Committee. By the 1970s, the speaker had effectively been restored as the de facto head of the Rules Committee, even though not a member. The term "the speaker's committee" highlights the reality of how partisan power considerations have shaped the majority party's legislative agenda and the procedures under which it is considered.

January 4, 2007, was a historic day in the US House of Representatives, as the 110th Congress convened. It was not so much that Democrats had regained control of the chamber after twelve years of Republican rule, as significant as that was, but that for the first time in House history a woman was about to become its speaker. Representative Nancy Pelosi, beginning her tenth term representing the San Francisco Bay Area of California, was poised to become the fifty-second speaker of the House.

Pelosi was literally born to politics; her father and brother, Thomas D'Alesandro Jr. and Thomas D'Alesandro III, had both been mayors of Baltimore. Her political genes traveled well to the West Coast, where she was first elected to the House in a special election in 1987 to fill the vacant seat left by the death of Representative Sala Burton, widow of the former House power broker Representative Phil Burton.

Pelosi rose rapidly in Democratic leadership ranks, elected first as Democratic whip in 2002 when Representative Dave Bonior of Michigan stepped down to run for governor of Michigan. Later that year, she was elected Democratic leader when Representative Dick Gephardt of Missouri gave up the post to run for president. Just four years later, Pelosi helped engineer the successful Democratic campaign to retake control of the House, making her the highest-ranking woman politician in the history of the country.

When the clerk completed a call of the roll, Pelosi was declared the winner over Republican leader John Boehner of Ohio on a predictable, party-line vote of 233–202. This set the stage for Boehner to perform the ceremonial duties of gaveling the House to order, introducing the new speaker, and turning the gavel over to Pelosi (along with a nontraditional, congratulatory peck on the cheek).

At the end of her acceptance speech, Pelosi invited all the children of members-elect in the chamber (including her own grandchildren) to join her on the rostrum before she was sworn in. More than three dozen children excitedly responded by swarming the podium to examine the gavel and share the moment with the grandmotherly about-to-be-speaker. Representative John Dingell of Michigan, the dean of the House, then administered the oath of office to Pelosi, who then swore in the rest of the members en masse.[1] The extra TV lights were then doused, the chamber emptied as most members hurried off to their ceremonial swearing-in pictures with the new speaker, and the galleries drained as visiting constituents hustled off to receptions in their representatives' offices.

The paucity of members on the floor and the reduced lighting in the chamber left the impression that the House was winding down, that it had completed all the important business of the day and only routine matters remained to be transacted. Nothing could be further from the truth. The House still had to debate and adopt its rules for the next two years. When there is a turnover in party control, as there was with the 2006 election results, that debate can be an important signal of the new majority's institutional and policy aspirations.

Although the House Rules Committee had not yet been formed, Democratic representative Louise Slaughter of New York was its presumptive chair and would become the first woman in history to lead the committee. Slaughter was recognized to offer a privileged resolution establishing a two-step process to adopt House rules for the new Congress. The purpose of the first resolution was simply to set up a process to allow for a separate debate and vote on the five separate titles of the second resolution, which contained the actual rule changes.[2] In parliamentary parlance, the first resolution was a special rule for considering the second resolution, adopting standing rules for the new House. This time, it came with a twist.

The broader purpose of the more expansive, two-step process in adopting rules was to highlight, through longer debates and more votes, the bold new directions Democrats were claiming to chart, which would allow all members greater opportunities to speak and vote on separate pieces of the package. They hoped even to encourage some bipartisan support for at least parts of the package, in contrast to what in the past had been a very partisan, slam-dunk exercise on opening day. The multistep process at least gave the appearance of greater openness and fairness.

Slaughter plunged right into why Democrats had regained control of the House. Because of a series of ethics scandals in the previous Congress in which Republican members accepted gifts and trips from lobbyists, she explained, "The culture of the last Congress came to be defined by a phrase now common to America. It was a 'culture of corruption.'" What was needed, she went on, was "for a new culture to take hold in Washington, a culture of commitment," and with it a "new legislative framework" of rules that will "keep the body focused on the well-being of the American people."[3]

House and Senate Democrats, under House Democratic leader Pelosi and Senate Democratic leader Harry Reid, had capitalized on the scandals by introducing the "Honest Leadership and Open Government Act" on February 1, 2006.[4] The rules package they presented in the House on opening day, a year later, incorporated at least modified versions of many of those reform proposals.

As the election grew closer, Pelosi and her House leadership colleagues unveiled what they called A New Direction for America. Their platform, called "Six for '06," promised laws that would provide real security at home and abroad, jobs, college access for all, energy independence, and affordable health care. The platform also included a congressional reform piece labeled "Honest Leadership and Open Government."[5] The platform was a clear knockoff of the GOP's 1994 Contract with America, with its commitments to House procedural and ethics reforms and a package of priority legislative bills. The main difference was that Democrats were pledging to complete votes on their "Six for '06" priority bills within one hundred hours, compared to the Republicans' one hundred–day contract timeline.

If imitation is the sincerest form of flattery, House Republicans should have been flattered. But they did not let on that they were. The Democrats had used the GOP's playbook to beat Republicans at their own game. This included charging their opponents with presiding over the most corrupt Congress ever, promising to return the institution to a clean House, and restoring the regular order to the legislative process.

The Republicans' contract package in 1995 included a host of House rules changes plus a ten-point platform of legislation they intended to pass during the first one hundred days, although this translated into roughly two dozen bills that were to be considered and reported from committees without amendment. Moreover, the bills were to be brought to the floor under fair and open debate.[6]

The Democrats' rules package in 2007 consisted of five titles, the first four of which dealt with rules changes, and a fifth title that dealt with the legislative commitments the Democrats had made to enact six bills in one hundred hours. Title I of the rules package simply adopted the rules of the previous Congress as the base text for the Democratic changes. Title II contained "Ethics Reforms," including bans on lobbyists' gifts to members; restrictions on lobbyist-paid travel for members; new travel authorization rules and public disclosure requirements; a ban on travel in corporate jets; and increased ethics training for members and staff.

Title III, "Civility," prohibited the speaker from holding votes open for longer than the scheduled time for the purpose of changing votes and required conference committees to operate in an open and fair manner. Both rules were in response to House Republicans holding open for three hours the final vote on the prescription drug bill in 2003 in order to pass the measure.

Title IV, "Fiscal Responsibility," prohibited budget reconciliation bills from increasing the deficit; required the publication by committees of lists of all earmarks and targeted tax benefits in their reported bills, and the names of members requesting them; and included a prohibition on trading earmarks for votes.

Title V, labeled "Miscellaneous," was summarized in a *Congressional Record* insert by Slaughter as allowing "for the consideration of several pieces of legislation that are part of the 'first 100 hours' agenda if special rules for those provisions are not separately reported."[7]

This latter title was the twist on the rules adoption resolution. Whereas the first four titles strictly addressed adopting standing rules for the House in the 110th Congress, the final title included four special rules (or order of business resolutions) for the consideration of four bills: (1) a bill to implement the recommendations of the National Commission on Terrorist Attacks on the US, (2) a bill to increase the federal minimum wage, (3) a bill to provide for embryonic stem cell research, and (4) a bill to allow the secretary of health and human services to negotiate lower covered Part D drug prices for Medicare beneficiaries. In addition, the title made in order consideration of a House resolution to enhance intelligence oversight authority.[8]

Under the terms of the special rule, all four legislative bills would be debatable for one hour and not subject to amendment. The minority would still be able to offer a final motion to recommit with instructions that could, if adopted, allow for a vote on a germane amendment.

The final two measures in the Democrats' "Six for '06" legislative platform were a college student relief act and a long-term energy alternatives bill. They would be considered under separate special rules granted by the Rules Committee in mid-January. As with the first four bills listed in the rules resolution, the final two would be considered without amendment and with just one hour of debate each.

The irony of this closed process was not lost on Republicans. The Democrats had pledged in their A New Direction for America manifesto that "bills should generally come to the floor under a procedure that allows open, full, and fair debate consisting of a full amendment process that grants the Minority the right to offer its alternatives." Yet right off the bat they were bringing their top-priority bills to the floor under procedures completely closed to any and all amendments.

Representative David Dreier of California, the top-ranking Rules Committee Republican, chided his new chairwoman-designate, Representative Slaughter, on these broken pledges immediately following her introductory remarks. "Now, . . . in spite of that great directive that came forward, we have a rules package that actually self-executes closed rules for bills that haven't even been introduced, and won't even be going through the committee process," Dreier observed. As for the Democrats' pledges of a more fair and open regular order, with guarantees of minority alternatives, Dreier concluded that "promises were made, and they are not being kept. . . . Unfortunately, this rules package shuts us out from the start."[9]

Dreier failed to mention (and Slaughter did not bother to mention) that Republicans had acted similarly on the opening day of the 104th Congress, although not on such a grand scale. The GOP rules package on January 4, 1995, also included a special rule for the consideration of an unreported bill, the so-called Congressional Accountability Act of 1995, which applied to Congress the same labor laws that apply to the private sector. On that occasion, the minority party Democrats twitted their Republican colleagues on breaking their openness pledge on day one, although Democrats later joined unanimously in voting for the bill itself.[10]

Fast-forwarding again to Speaker Pelosi's opening day in 2007, the Republicans vociferously reminded the Democrats of their commitment when in the minority to restore minority rights in the House if elected to the majority. They resurrected a document that Minority Leader Pelosi had unveiled to great fanfare on May 5, 2006, titled "New House Principles: A Congress for All Americans." According to the accompanying press release, the

Democrats were pledging to restore democracy in the "People's House" by guaranteeing that the voices of the people are heard.

Their statement of principles was broken into two parts: "Bipartisan Administration of the House" and "Regular Order for Legislation." The first part included calling for regular consultation among the party and committee leaders of the two parties over the scheduling, administration, and operations of the House. It also called for allocating one-third of committee budgets and office space to the minority party.

The second part of the Democrats' announced principles in 2006 included such procedural reforms as fully opening committee hearings and meetings with twenty-four-hour advance availability of bills before markup; allowing for open, full, and fair floor debates that include a full amendment process; enforcing strict time limits on floor votes; and holding weekly meetings of House-Senate conference committees with full opportunity for input and debate.[11]

For the purposes of the January 4, 2007, debate, House Republicans transformed these principles into actual rules changes they proposed to offer if the House defeated the previous question on House Resolution 5. Predictably, however, the previous question was adopted on a party-line vote, 222–197.[12]

Dreier then offered a motion to commit the Democrats' rules package to a select committee consisting of the majority and minority leaders with instructions to report back "forthwith" (immediately) with an amendment prohibiting the Rules Committee from reporting any special rule waiving points of order against requirements for roll call votes on appropriations, budget, and tax measures, and requiring a three-fifths vote for any bill or amendment increasing income tax rates. That Republican motion also went down on a party-line vote.[13]

When House Resolution 6, the resolution adopting House rules and providing for the consideration of four major bills, was called up, each of its five titles was given a separate debate, but minority

Republicans were allowed just one motion to commit at the end of the fifth title.

Representative Paul Ryan (R-WI), as a member of the Ways and Means Committee, was designated by the GOP leadership to offer the motion to recommit. It provided for consideration of a bill improving access by small business entrepreneurs to health plans for their employees, and of a rule to ban the practice of earmarking projects for members in legislation. Again, the minority motion was turned back along party lines.[14]

The Speaker's Committee

As noted in chapter 1, one of Speaker Thomas Reed's little known legacies as speaker was instituting in 1895 a relatively closed, majority-controlled process for adopting House rules on the opening day of a new Congress. Previously, the House would either adopt the rules of the prior Congress or wait for the Rules Committee to report any changes in those rules. The resolution to adopt the rules would then be debated and amended under an open process. As historian George Galloway points out in his history of the House: "The customary practice in *post bellum* days was to proceed under general parliamentary law, often for several days, with unlimited debate, until a satisfactory revision of former rules had been effected. Proposed changes in the old rules were discussed on these occasions in a leisurely, good-natured way and the meaning of the complex code of the House was explained to the new Members."[15] Galloway goes on to note that on three occasions after the rules revision of 1880 "two months or more elapsed before the amended code was finally adopted, in striking contrast to the celerity with which the old rules have been rushed through in recent times."[16]

The House has Reed to thank for modern-day "celerity" in rulemaking when a new Congress convenes. Even when there has been a turnover in party control—as happened in 1995, 2007, and 2011—and the new majority has extended debate time and allowed for separate votes on its rules packages, the minority has been confined to three procedural motions: (1) a motion at the outset to refer the rules package to a select committee with instructions; (2) the motion for the previous question, which if defeated allows the minority to control an extra hour and offer any germane amendments of its choosing; and (3) a motion to commit the rules resolution to a select committee with instructions to report back immediately with specified amendments.

The third option, a motion to commit to a select committee with amendatory instructions, was first employed in modern times on an opening day rules package in 1981 by House Republican leader Bob Michel, with instructions to report back within one day. Beginning in 1989, the motion was changed by the Republicans so that the instructions were to commit to a select committee, which was to report back "forthwith"—that is, immediately—with the specified rules changes.[17]

Neither the previous question motion nor the committal motion is subject to debate. As seen in this chapter's case study from 2007, those procedural motions are usually turned back on partisan votes, thereby depriving the minority of any direct votes on its preferred rules changes. That is because both motions involve a two-step process: first, adopting the motion; and second, if successful, then offering the minority party's amendatory changes.

Majority control of the modern rules adoption process nearly slipped away from the majority Republicans on the opening day of the 61st Congress in 1909 when a small group of insurgent Republicans joined with the minority Democrats to defeat the majority's resolution to readopt the rules of the previous Congress, even though the majority had prevailed in adopting the previous question.

Democratic minority leader Champ Clark of Missouri was then recognized to offer an alternative rules resolution, which would have established a fifteen-member Rules Committee (versus the existing five members), with names specified in the resolution. Because Speaker Joe Cannon's name was not among those named, he would have been effectively removed as both a member of the committee and its chairman. The new committee, in addition to exercising the existing duties of the Rules Committee, would be charged with reporting any further changes in House rules by the first week in December 1909. At only one point in his remarks did Clark at least indirectly characterize what was objectionable about Speaker Cannon, saying that if members did not vote to remove him from the Rules Committee they could not go home "whining" to their constituents that the reason they did not get things done they wished to "was because the Speaker of this House was such an infernal despot."[18]

In a surprise twist, the House then defeated the previous question on Clark's resolution, meaning the chair could then recognize someone leading the opposition to Clark's motion.[19] The speaker recognized Representative John Fitzgerald (D-NY), chief of the Tammany Hall delegation in Congress. Cannon had worked out a compromise with Fitzgerald to head off the effort to remove the speaker from control of the Rules Committee. The Fitzgerald substitute established a unanimous consent calendar for bringing up bills not reported by committees, strengthened the Calendar Wednesday rule for bringing up bills reported by committees but not cleared by the Rules Committee, and permitted a motion to recommit on any bill with precedence given to a member opposed to the bill.[20] As Fitzgerald explained, "Mr. Speaker, for ten years I have been endeavoring to have this House vote down the previous question upon the motion to adopt rules . . . because . . . I was convinced there were some abuses in the procedure of the House which should be corrected. I would consider myself as nothing less than a blithering idiot if, after clamoring here for ten years, I was unable to suggest a single remedy for the abuses against which I complain."[21]

Speaker Cannon dodged the Democratic bullet for the moment by helping to engineer Fitzgerald's successful substitute rules package. Yet public sentiment, combined with internal House discontent with Cannon's leadership, continued to grow. Cannon did not anticipate one of his own party members taking another stab at changing the rules a year later, in the second session of that same Congress. Insurgent Republican George Norris of Nebraska managed to do exactly that, using a precedent Cannon established the day before to hoist the speaker with his own petard.

Paving the way for successful revolt against Cannon was the speaker's attempt in mid-March 1910 to recognize the chairman of the Census Committee to call up an amendment to the census bill without first disposing of the call of committees under the recently adopted Calendar Wednesday reform. When a point of order was raised against the move, Cannon overruled it on grounds that the census provision was a matter of constitutional privilege given Congress's responsibility to provide for taking a decennial census, on the basis of which the allocation of House seats by state would be determined.

On appeal, the House overturned the speaker's ruling. However, when the census bill was brought up the following day as a matter of constitutional privilege, a point of order was again raised. Cannon dutifully upheld the point of order based on his rebuke by the House the previous day. Having made their point about protecting Calendar Wednesday, the House was prepared to reverse the speaker and allow the census bill to go forward.

This did not go unnoticed by Norris, who seized on the constitutional privilege precedent to call up a resolution changing House rules to alter the composition of the Rules Committee. Norris's resolution would replace the five-member committee appointed by the speaker with a fifteen-member committee with one majority member elected from each of nine groupings of states, and one minority member elected from each of six groupings of states.

Majority Leader John Dalzell (R-PA) raised a point of order that the resolution was not privileged under the Constitution, and that only the Rules Committee could report changes in House rules that were privileged on the floor. Cannon allowed debate on the point of order to go on for three days before he finally ruled in favor of the point of order. Norris appealed the ruling of the chair, and the House refused to sustain Cannon's ruling, 162–182. Debate then proceeded on Norris's resolution. He had been persuaded by Democrats to drop the regional groupings and reduce the size of the Rules Committee from fifteen to ten members elected by the House, none of whom could be the speaker. The House then adopted Norris's resolution, as amended, 191–156.

Cannon offered to entertain a motion that the speakership be vacated (that the czar speaker be dethroned), and a Democratic member obliged. Because insurgent Republicans were not about to turn control of the House over to the Democrats, the motion was defeated. However, as Cannon readily admitted, "Cannonism was dead." Although the speaker retained the right to appoint other committees, even this changed in the following Congress when the Democrats took control and adopted a rule that all committees would be elected by the House.[22]

Cannon was at least vindicated on his way out the door as speaker at the end of the historic 61st Congress. On January 9, 1911, during the third session of Congress, Representative Charles Fuller, a Republican from Illinois, relying on the Norris precedent, rose to offer a change in House rules, which he said was privileged under the Constitution. Representative James Mann, also an Illinois Republican (who would become his party's leader in the next Congress), raised a point of order against the resolution. Apparently relishing a revisiting of the issue, Cannon let debate on the point of order proceed at some length.

Representative Oscar Underwood of Alabama, who would become the Democrats' majority leader in the next Congress, said he had never argued that Cannon's earlier ruling was wrong.

He said the speaker's ruling nevertheless had to be overturned in 1910 because the American people wanted a divorce between Cannon and the Rules Committee and that was the only way to do it. Mann and Underwood went around on whether he was following up on the revolution or returning to the old order. Underwood replied that further revolution was not necessary because the will of the House was no longer being thwarted.

Instead of following the precedent that overthrew him, Cannon sustained the point of order that Fuller's motion to change the rules from the floor was not in order. Fuller said he would not appeal the decision of the chair "out of great respect for the Speaker, . . . and realizing his great knowledge of parliamentary law, his absolute honesty and fairness in deciding all questions in accordance with his best judgment." Nevertheless, Representative Joseph Gaines, a Republican from West Virginia, did appeal the ruling, and the House upheld Cannon, 235–53, with 96 members not voting and 3 members voting "present."

Among those upholding Cannon's ruling this time were top Democrats Champ Clark and Oscar Underwood, as well as Republican Fuller, who had raised the issue. Whether the whole episode was a setup to salve Cannon's wounded pride is difficult to prove. But the outcome did provide a fitting end to a turbulent chapter in House history—one that preserved the ability of the House to function in an orderly fashion.[23]

Although the revolt and its immediate aftermath removed the speaker's direct control over the Rules Committee as its chairman, it also cemented the sole authority of the committee for reporting privileged resolutions changing House rules once it was formed. Individual members could no longer, willy-nilly, claim floor time to offer their preferred rules changes.

The 1910 revolt against Cannon removed the speaker forever as a member and chairman of the Rules Committee. However, in times of strong party cohesion, the committee has again become known as "the Speaker's Committee," whether under Speaker

Gingrich or Speaker Pelosi. Both of these speakers played a central role in creating and passing the opening day rules packages when their respective parties retook control of the House.

Moreover, as Congress has become more partisan and polarized, as has been the case at the turn of both the twentieth and twenty-first centuries, the minority party has used the opening day rules adoption exercise as an opportunity to air its complaints about majority party rule, quite often in the form of an alternative rules package. The struggles over House rules and over control of the Rules Committee have been microcosms of the larger historical changes that have shaped the House over the last 228 years.

3

Procedural Triage for
Health Care Reform

PRESIDENT BARACK OBAMA'S SIGNATURE legislation in his first term, health care reform, was finally enacted in 2010 as the Affordable Care Act. In the face of strong partisan opposition to the legislation, Obama and the Democratic Congress were able to secure its enactment without Republican support. Their success flew in the face of the conventional wisdom that Congress could not pass major legislation without bipartisan support. The Obama health care saga is a textbook demonstration of the majority party pulling out all the stops to control the levers of power in Congress to achieve victory against extreme odds. It stands in stark contrast to the failure of the Clinton health care effort in the 103rd Congress, which is also recounted briefly here.

Despite the expectation that voters would reward the Democrats at the polls for their new health care benefit, Democrats lost control of the House in the ensuing 2010 elections, and they lost control of the Senate four years later. The takeaway lesson was that not all partisan power plays are richly rewarded. When the public is not able to follow the convoluted debates, comprehend the benefits, or

38

follow the confusing procedural path such legislation must take, voter doubts may arm the minority party with sharp weapons for the next electoral battle.

On January 6, 2009, Nancy Pelosi was sworn in for the second time as House speaker. In her acceptance speech, she called attention to the historic significance of the election of Barack Obama as the forty-fourth president of the United States, and the need for Congress and the country to work with him to "fulfill the rest of America's promise." She continued: "All of that promise, will not be redeemed quickly or easily, but it must be pursued urgently, with spirited debate and without partisan deadlock or delay."

She then spelled out the urgent problems to be addressed— a sneak preview of Obama's inaugural address and first-term agenda—the economic recession with its massive job losses; the lack of adequate health care coverage; the states' financial crises; climate change; and conflicts abroad, including terrorist threats that could eventually strike home. She punctuated each crisis enumerated with the refrain "We need action, and we need action now."

On health care, she observed that "families and children without health care, and millions more who fear losing coverage or who are facing rising costs, cannot afford to wait any longer."[1] Once again, she called upon the dean of the House (by virtue of being the longest-serving member), Representative John Dingell Jr., to administer to her the oath of office.

Eight months later, Dingell would again be singled out in the House Chamber, this time by President Barack Obama during a health care address to a joint session of Congress. Obama noted that though he was not the first president to take up the cause of health care—that had been Theodore Roosevelt nearly a century earlier—"I am determined to be the last." Obama elaborated that, ever since Roosevelt, nearly every president and every Congress, whether Democrat or Republican, "has attempted to meet this challenge in some way." A bill for comprehensive health care "was first introduced by John Dingell Sr. in 1943," Obama noted, and "sixty-five years later, his son continues to introduce that same bill at the beginning of each session."[2]

Obama went on to express concern over the threat posed by partisan deadlock and delay. Although recognizing that progress was being made in developing a consensus health care bill, and that there was agreement "on about 80 percent of what needs to be done," the president added that what has happened over the last few months "is the same partisan spectacle that only hardens the disdain many Americans have toward their own government." And, he elaborated, "too many have used this as an opportunity to score short-term political points, even if it robs the country of our opportunity to solve a long-term challenge. And out of this blizzard of charges and countercharges, confusion has reigned." Throwing down the gauntlet, the president told Congress that "the time for bickering is over. The time for games has passed. Now is the season for action. . . . Now is the time to deliver on health care."[3]

Still, it would be almost seven more months before a bill was completed and signed into law on March 23, 2010. At the signing ceremony in the East Room of the White House, the president noted the long journey health care reform had taken: "Today, after almost a century of trying, today, after over a year of debate, today, after all the votes have been tallied—health insurance reform becomes law in the United States of America."

Even the president seemed a little astounded that they had pulled it off: "Our presence here today is remarkable and improbable. With all the punditry, all of the lobbying, all of the game-playing that passes for governing in Washington, it's been easy at times to doubt our ability to do such a thing. . . . It's easy to succumb to the sense of cynicism about what's possible in this country."

But the president was quick to share credit (and nineteen signing pens) with those both inside and outside Congress and the administration who had been central to passing the legislation, specifically praising Representative Dingell and the late Senator Ted Kennedy, both of whom had literally devoted their lives to the cause; and "all of the terrific committee chairs [five in all], and all the members of Congress who did what was difficult, but did what was right, and passed health care reform." He extended accolades for their efforts to "one of the best speakers the House of Representatives has ever had, Speaker Nancy Pelosi (Audience: *Nancy! Nancy! Nancy! Nancy!*)"; and "one of the best majority leaders the Senate has ever had, Mr. Harry Reid (*Applause*)."[4]

How the health care reform bill made it into law is a long and winding saga with procedural twists and turns engineered by party and committee leaders on both sides to facilitate its success or failure. Moreover, the death of Democratic senator Ted Kennedy in August 2009, and his replacement the following January by Republican senator Scott Brown, deprived Majority Leader Harry Reed of his previous filibuster-proof sixty-seat majority, necessitating new tactical maneuvers. When one considers that not a single Republican supported the final bill in the Senate, and only one member did in the House, the president's characterizing of it as an "improbable" success story is understatement at its finest.

Lessons of the Past

It became apparent from the outset of the Obama administration that the president did not want to repeat the mistakes of the past—namely, the failed Clinton health care initiative in the 103rd Congress (1993–94). That legislation, the product of a secretive White House task force headed by then First Lady Hillary Clinton, included key cabinet members and White House staff but excluded important players such as doctors, insurers, and members of Congress (although more than a hundred Democratic staffers from relevant congressional committees were included in fifteen working groups that fed information to the task force).[5]

The Clinton task force product was presented to Congress in almost a take it or leave it fashion, raising the hackles even of congressional leaders of the president's own party. Congress ultimately chose to leave it rather than take it due to an inability to muster majority votes for either the president's bill or any variations reported by any of the committees of jurisdiction. Neither chamber even dared to bring a bill to a floor vote before the 103rd Congress adjourned. The House Energy and Commerce Committee, headed by Dingell, was not even able to report a bill, although the House Ways and Means compensated by reporting two bills as the price of getting anything out.

Obama, by contrast, made sure that all the affected interests were in the room when the reform plan was being crafted, and that all the interests involved would benefit in some way from the final product recommended to Congress and, thus, would heartily support it. Moreover, the president was careful not to appear to dictate the details of the plan to Congress. Instead, he patiently—up to a point—supported free-flowing negotiations on Capitol Hill.

The downside to the tactic was that widely disparate approaches could and did emerge from the two chambers, making their reconciliation a steep challenge. The House, in November 2009, and the Senate, in December 2009, passed bills that seemed to defy any prospect of compromise. As year two rolled around, the president was being widely criticized for a lack of leadership on the issue by members of his own party, even though that was clearly part of his game plan.

Smart presidents wait for strategic moments to intervene and close deals rather than engage in constant, intrusive meddling. In reality, Obama's key staff members—especially the White House's health policy czar, Nancy Parle—were in daily contact with their Hill counterparts. The president himself would begin playing an increasing behind-the-scenes role as his patience wore thin.

Congress, too, was careful to avoid repeating past mistakes in dealing with major health care legislation. Obviously, President Clinton's earlier failed health care reform effort in the Congress was front and center as the poster child for how not to proceed at either end of Pennsylvania Avenue.

A Long and Winding Road

The health care bill process began, as do other major pieces of legislation, with drafting and introduction by key players in both houses. In the House of Representatives, Speaker Pelosi was anxious to ensure at the outset that the three major committees involved—Energy and Commerce, Ways and Means, and Education and Labor—began on the same page. The chairpersons of these three committees—respectively, representatives Henry Waxman (CA), Charles Rangel (NY), and George Miller (CA)—cemented their commitment to work from the same bill in a letter to President Obama in mid-March 2009.[6]

The effort would entail careful, behind the scenes negotiations in the Democratic caucus to forge a unified draft. On July 14, 2009, the leadership-backed bill, weighing in at more than one thousand pages, was introduced as "America's Affordable Health Choices Act of 2009" (HR 3200), with Representative John Dingell (the former Energy and Commerce Committee chairman) fittingly designated as the lead sponsor.

The chairpersons of the three committees appeared next on the introduced bill as the principal cosponsors. As Waxman explains in an epilogue to his 2009 book, published a year later, "Rangel, Miller and I agreed to give Dingell the honor of putting his name among the authors and introducing it in the House." Waxman adds that he and his two cohorts took the "novel" approach of cooperating this time around because all three had experienced failure in the past by not doing so. One of the reasons things failed under President Clinton's administration "was because the committees produced competing bills and never settled on one," Waxman recounts. "We knew this could be our last opportunity to achieve our goal."

Although Waxman notes at the outset of his account that the two-year endeavor "was a model of congressional leadership," he makes clear that the pivotal leadership role was played by the three chairpersons. They met regularly, along with key aides, first to draft a blueprint and then to fashion a single bill.[7]

The two main goals of a health care reform bill laid out by Obama during his campaign were ensuring universal coverage and reducing the overall costs of care. Consequently, the bills produced by the House and Senate required most people to obtain basic health insurance or pay a penalty.

To achieve this, most employers, except for small businesses, were mandated to offer coverage to their employees or pay a fee. Assistance would be provided to small businesses otherwise not able to afford coverage for their employees. Those unable to obtain coverage from employers would be able to choose policies from state-based exchanges or marketplaces and receive subsidies for the cost of their premiums. Insurers would be required to offer a basic benefit package, and they would be prohibited from imposing annual or lifetime limits on coverage, from denying coverage to those with preexisting conditions, and from terminating coverage of those who got sick.

The main points of controversy emerged over whether to provide a "public option" or a government-run system to compete with private insurers and thus presumably to keep costs low; whether to tighten abortion restrictions already in existence for federally funded programs; how to fund the new program's benefits; and whether to expand Medicaid coverage for the poor to a wider range of low-income persons.[8]

The House Ways and Means Committee and the Education and Labor Committee met to consider the bill just two days after its introduction, with the former committee reporting it on a 23–18 vote on July 17. Only three Democrats defected on the vote to report, following a sixteen-hour markup to consider amendments. The Education and Labor Committee reported its version the same day, 26–22, again with 3 Democrats joining all Republicans in opposition.

As Waxman explains in his book, the task of the Energy and Commerce Committee was more difficult because it had both liberal and conservative Democratic members. These included seven members of the Blue Dog Democrats—a conservative caucus of rural and southern Democrats "who worried greatly about government spending." Waxman's committee was far more representative of the House at large, and consequently he thought that "whatever we passed would carry significant weight." But this also made the process of reporting a bill "a terrible grind."

At one point, Waxman recounts, he was so frustrated by resistance from the Blue Dog Democrats that he "almost stormed out," threatening to take the bill to the Rules Committee for a floor rule, without a committee report. But his staff director helped avert a walkout. Ultimately, Waxman says, the speaker, majority leader, and the president all became involved in negotiating a final compromise that lowered the costs of the bill by reducing subsidies and providing a weaker public option. These developments, in turn, sparked a revolt among liberals, who threatened "to blow the whole thing up."[9] Nevertheless, Energy and Commerce completed its work on July 31, ordering the bill reported on a 31–28 vote.

Among the concessions made to the Blue Dog Democrats was that no floor votes would occur before the August recess. This interlude would be needed anyway to negotiate compromises between the three versions of HR 3200 and to obtain the Congressional Budget Office's scoring of the final bill. The three committees waited until October 14 to file reports on their differing versions. Two weeks later, on October 29, a negotiated compromise between the three versions was introduced as a new bill, the "Affordable Health Care for America Act" (HR 3962), again with Dingell as lead sponsor and the three committee chairs as prime cosponsors. Running nearly two thousand pages, the measure was unveiled at a rally of House Democrats on the Capitol steps.

In the Senate, the two major committees—Health, Education, Labor, and Pensions (HELP); and Finance—went their own ways on separate bills, with Finance dealing with Medicare, Medicaid, and revenues, and HELP with the rest. The HELP bill, under the direction of the acting chairman, Senator Chris Dodd (CT), in Kennedy's absence due to illness, was first out of the box, with the committee completing action on its draft on a 13–10 party-line vote. That followed an extensive markup process with almost five hundred amendments offered; of those, close to 160 Republican amendments were adopted. The measure would later be introduced by Senator Tom Harkin on September 19 as "The Affordable Health Choices Act" (S 1679).

The Senate Finance Committee took considerably longer to produce its bill, as Chairman Max Baucus of Montana made a concerted effort to forge a bipartisan compromise. The attempt eventually collapsed when all three Republicans on the so-called Gang of Six withdrew from participation. Consequently, Finance did not complete its work until October 13, after seven days of debate. The bill, reported on a 14–9 vote, was titled "America's Healthy Future Act" (S 1796) and was formally introduced by Baucus on October 19, 2009.[10]

The complexities and controversies joined in such a massive piece of legislation presented a puzzle of moving parts, not unlike a Rubik's cube, that the committee chairs, party leaders, and members of both chambers would manipulate for months before arriving at an acceptable, albeit not perfectly aligned, solution. In Congress, it is not as important that all the policy pieces fit nicely together as it is that the political pieces click in place for a winning outcome. The not so secret code numbers to crack the cube in each chamber are 218 in the House (a simple majority) and 60 in the Senate (votes needed to end a filibuster), and that is where leadership intervention is critical, even if it means upsetting finely wrought compromises hammered out at the committee level.

The House Democratic leadership's meld of the three disparate committee health bills into its newly minted bill (HR 3962) set the stage for House Rules Committee action on November 6 during a twelve-hour marathon hearing and contentious markup. The Republicans forced sixteen roll call votes on various motions, either to postpone consideration or to broaden the proposed rule to include more amendments—all of which were rejected on party-line votes.

The House had remained in recess late into the evening and early morning hours solely to allow the Rules Committee to file its rule when ready. The committee eventually did so at 2:25 A.M. on November 7, after which the House adjourned the "legislative day" of November 6.[11]

The special rule (H. Res. 903) setting the procedural ground rules for considering the health care reform bill was complex. In addition to making in order consideration of the new health care bill, it made in order another bill, the "Medicare Physician Payment Reform Act" (HR 3961). The portion of the rule for the physicians' payment bill was a closed rule (no amendments), with one hour of general debate.

The health care reform bill portion of the rule provided for four hours of general debate followed by four amendments, the first two of which were on automatic pilot, otherwise known as a "self-executing rule," using the following language: "The amendment printed in part A of the report of the Committee on Rules accompanying this resolution, perfected by the modification printed in part B of such report, shall be considered as adopted." That was the tip-off that further compromises had been drafted right up until the day before floor consideration.

The Rules Committee's report on the rule referred to the Part A amendment as "the manager's amendment" and carried Representative Dingell's name. The text of the Dingell amendment, running fifteen pages in the Rules Committee report, made numerous changes throughout the underlying bill, from pages 17 to 1,977.

The Part B amendment was confined primarily to additional money for establishing medical schools in underserved areas and providing incentives for public health workers to serve in such areas. The self-executing device for such amendments ensured they would not be subject to a separate debate and vote during consideration of the bill itself. (For data on self-executing rules over time, see tables 2 and 3 in the appendix.)

The rule also made in order an abortion amendment, if offered by Democratic representative Bart Stupak of Ohio, and a Republican substitute, if offered by Republican leader John Boehner. Finally, the rule provided for one motion to recommit, with or without instructions—a final opportunity for the minority to amend the bill.

Rules Committee chair Louise Slaughter called up the rule on the House floor at 10:43 A.M. on Saturday, November 7, with Dingell presiding as speaker pro tempore over the hour of debate. Not coincidentally, he had also presided over the Medicare debate some forty-four years earlier. Although the majority is recognized for the entire one hour of debate allowed on the rule, the majority manager traditionally yields half that time to the manager for the Rules Committee minority, in this case Republican representative Pete Sessions of Texas.

The debate on the rule was unusually disjointed, as scores of members lined up at both party tables to seek unanimous consent to insert their prepared remarks in the *Congressional Record*. Contrary to the House rules prohibiting embellishments to such requests, the members purposely included either positive or negative characterizations of the bill, forcing Dingell to repeatedly admonish members (and eventually charge time consumed against the rule's managers).

Ultimately, the rule was adopted, 242–192. Only two specific complaints were raised against the procedure, both concerning the late availability of the self-executing amendment language. The bill went on to pass the House that same day, 220–215, after the Stupak abortion amendment was agreed to and the Republican substitute was rejected.

Mike Lux, a former Clinton administration official involved with the 1993–94 health care effort, praised the Democratic leadership's floor operation to secure passage. "On the final vote," he observed, "the whipping process was intense and impressive. Democratic leaders I have known in the past have rarely played this kind of hardball, but some kneecaps were broken Saturday night to get these votes."[12]

The health care reform process in 2009–10 enabled the Democratic leadership to showcase its full kit of procedural tools. In addition to the initial special rule, and later a second special rule to resolve differences between the houses, the leadership used budget reconciliation—a deficit reduction process set in motion by the annual budget resolution—to produce revenue or entitlement changes to help achieve the budget resolution's bottom-line numbers. The House budget resolution for fiscal year 2010 contained instructions to report language both on health care reform and student loans. The Senate budget resolution did not contain instructions. Both Senate Finance chairman Max Baucus (MT) and Budget chairman Kent Conrad (ND) vociferously opposed using reconciliation for health care on grounds it would ignite partisan passions and subvert the original intent of reconciliation. In Conrad's words, "I don't believe reconciliation was ever intended for this purpose."[13]

Because debate time on reconciliation bills is limited to twenty hours under the Budget Act, they cannot be filibustered in the Senate. That makes the process an especially tempting path for thorny political and partisan priorities. Conrad was outvoted by his Senate colleagues in conference committee so that reconciliation instructions were included in the final budget resolution, thereby keeping the option alive for future use if needed. As it turned out, they were needed.

Just as Speaker Pelosi and her leadership team and the three committee chairs had to forge a compromise bill for floor consideration (with the help of the Rules Committee), Senate majority leader Harry Reid was left to cobble a compromise from the Finance and HELP committees. Similar to the House effort, it would take more than one try. Instead of using the House-passed bill to graft on a Senate compromise, Reid chose a minor, unrelated, and noncontroversial House-passed bill, the "Service Members Homeownership Tax Act" (HR 3590), as the vehicle for the health care bill. He probably did so to reassure skittish senators who did not want to go near the House-passed health care bill with its controversial public option to compete with private insurance plans.

After extensive consultations with all Democratic senators, many more than once, Reid developed an amendment in the nature of a substitute (Senate Amendment 2786), which he offered to the House-passed service members tax bill on November 21, 2009. (It had taken two days and a cloture motion just to proceed to the consideration of the bill.) It would take more than another month and dozens of additional changes that Reid offered as a "manager's amendment" (Senate Amendment 3276) to his original substitute on December 18. Reid was then able to invoke cloture on the final amendment, 60–40, and secure Senate adoption, 60–39, on December 21 and 22, 2009, in time to still get home for Christmas—barely.

Republicans were able to force further delays by insisting that Reid's "manager's amendment" be read in its entirety, and by offering nondebatable amendments once the thirty hours of postcloture debate ended. It was not until December 24, Christmas Eve, that the Senate was able to finally pass its health care bill, 60–39.[14]

A Fork in the Road

Because the health care bills passed by the House and Senate differed in so many respects, reconciling their differences posed a challenge. House Democrats bristled at the thought of having to accept the Senate-passed bill, and Senate Democrats knew they could not hold their fragile sixty-vote coalition if forced to accept some of the House-passed bill's more liberal provisions. Then, the unthinkable happened. Reid's filibuster-proof Senate Democratic majority vanished when Republican candidate Scott Brown beat his Democratic opponent, Massachusetts attorney general Martha Coakley, in the January 19, 2010, special election to fill the seat left vacant by the death of Senator Ted Kennedy the previous August.

With the fate of the health bill hanging in a precarious balance, Democratic leaders were forced to change gears and engage in new thinking. Going to conference with the House would require not one but three cloture votes just to get to conference, let alone to overcome a filibuster of any final conference agreement. To finesse both House and Senate Democrats' reluctance to even be seen considering the other chamber's bill, the reconciliation strategy was activated.

The strategy's implementation required the House Ways and Means Committee and Education and Labor Committee to report their health care related budgetary pieces to the House Budget Committee. The Budget Committee was then obligated to combine them in a single bill, without change, and send it to the House Rules Committee for floor clearance.

As this occurred, the House would also provide a process to accept the Senate-passed bill (holding its nose), and then use its reconciliation bill to provide enough liberal fixes from its own original bill to appease House Democratic members. At the center of this maneuvering was the majority leadership, the key committee chairs, and the leadership's reliable procedural arm—the House Rules Committee.

Once passed by the House, the Senate-passed bill would be sent on to the president. Presumably the reconciliation cleanup bill would not be far behind once the Senate mustered the fifty votes needed (plus the vice president, if necessary) to clear this bill for the president's signature.

The only possible glitch, which made Budget Committee chairmen Senator Ken Conrad and Representative John Spratt nervous, was the "Byrd rule" prohibiting extraneous (nonbudgetary) matters from being included in reconciliation. A point of order sustained against any such provisions would result in that provision being dropped (unless a sixty-vote waiver could be secured in the Senate) and force the measure back to the other body for reconsideration.

"The Reconciliation Act of 2010" (HR 4872) was reported by the House Budget Committee March 17, 2010, on recommendations submitted by the Ways and Means and Education and Labor committees in October 2009. Although the Energy and Commerce Committee had also received reconciliation instructions, it did not report its recommendations. In such cases, the Budget Act authorizes the Rules Committee to fill in the blanks.

The measure's provisions both on health care and student loans were carefully scrutinized and vetted by the House and Senate parliamentarians' offices, Budget and Congressional Budget Office staff members, and others for any potential Byrd rule violations. Although the Budget Committee was required to package and report the bill as sent to it by the instructed committees, it was not precluded from suggesting further amendments to the Rules Committee for inclusion in the package, and, in this instance, it proposed numerous additional changes.

In devising a special rule for the two-bill package—the Senate health care reform amendment to the House-passed servicemen's tax bill (HR 3590) and the House-reported reconciliation bill (HR 4278)—the House leadership devised a no-pain way of disposing of the Senate amendment and sending it to the president without requiring a direct vote on the matter. The special rule would simply self-execute, or "deem" the adoption of the Senate amendment and passage of the House bill as amended. This would spare Democratic members who abhorred the Senate version from taking responsibility for it. After adoption of the rule (and with it the Senate health care amendment), the House could then proceed to consider the reconciliation bill.

The strategy became known among opponents as "the Slaughter Solution," after the Rules Committee chairwoman, Louise Slaughter, who reportedly championed the approach. When the proposed strategy was made public on March 15, Pelosi said, "I like it because people don't have to vote on the Senate bill." House majority leader Steny Hoyer backed her up. By using the "deem-and-pass" ploy, Hoyer said Democrats were "playing it straight" because the practice of self-executing the adoption of amendments was common.

A day later Hoyer's office issued a release quoting several prominent political scientists who charged Republicans with "hypocrisy" for criticizing a practice they had used when in the majority. The release also cited a column I had published in 2006 citing data showing the GOP use of the practice was even worse than under majority Democrats (see tables 2 and 3 in the appendix). Hoyer's release did not mention that I had consistently condemned the practice as antideliberative.[15]

Notwithstanding Hoyer's defense, opponents of the bill, both inside and outside the beltway, went ballistic at the perceived absurdity of enacting a law without voting on it. As the political scientist Barbara Sinclair describes it, the "Slaughter Solution" became "a cause célèbre" of conservatives on the airwaves.[16]

On February 25, 2010, at the Blair House summit on health care reform, Pelosi responded to criticism of the procedural shortcuts that had been used to pass the legislation to date: "Those people sitting at the kitchen table . . . don't want to hear about process. They want to hear about results." Shortly after the "Slaughter

Solution" was floated, an Associated Press photo published by ABC News told another story. There, in an audience of placard-waving seniors, at a "Kill the Bill" rally in Indianapolis being addressed by Representative Mike Pence (R-IN), was one poster that read " 'SLAUGHTER SOLUTION' Amend a Law That Doesn't Exist By Passing a Bill Without Voting On It!" Clearly, this was an instance in which at least a portion of an aroused public understood the nexus between procedure and policy—and did not like what it was seeing.[17]

As I went on to opine in the 2010 column, the self-executing process had only been used six times in a century to send a measure to the president at the final stage of the bill process without a final vote; most uses were for amendments at the initial stage of the bill process: "To equate the two scenarios isn't comparing apple and oranges. It's the difference between eating an apple and swallowing a watermelon whole."[18] Because the public uproar was so great, causing even some House Democrats to threaten to vote against such a rule, the leadership withdrew the idea before it got to the Rules Committee's doorstep. The "Slaughter Solution" had become the "Pelosi Problem," and it was not one the speaker relished while working to secure the necessary votes on the bills themselves.

In the end, the process used by the House Rules Committee at the final stage for the bills closely resembled the earlier events in November: a weekend Rules meeting, scores of members testifying, and dozens of amendments filed, self-executing language, a late night filing of the rule, and early morning consideration of it. The Rules Committee met for thirteen and half hours and heard testimony from twenty-seven House members pleading for their amendments, none of which were adopted.

Under the terms of the rule (H. Res. 1203), the Senate health care reform amendments to the House servicemen's tax bill (HR 3590) and the House reconciliation bill (HR 4872) would be debated together for two hours, followed by a motion by the majority leader or a designee to concur in the Senate amendments to the former bill, without further amendment. If that motion to concur was adopted, the House would then take up the reconciliation bill with the amendment printed in part A of the Rules Committee report, modified by the amendment printed in part B of the report—the so-called reconciliation fixes, or corrections—to be "considered as adopted." Although those amendments would not be subject to further amendment, the minority would be guaranteed one motion to recommit, with or without instructions (a final amendment to the bill).[19]

Rules Committee chairwoman Slaughter called up the rule on Sunday, March 21, shortly after 2 P.M. Before debate could begin on the rule, however, Budget Committee ranking Republican Paul Ryan of Wisconsin raised a point of order against consideration of the rule on grounds that the rule violated section 426(a) of the Budget Act by waiving points of order against the reconciliation bill relating to unfunded mandates.

The speaker pro tempore sustained the point of order, entitling Ryan and an opponent to ten minutes each on the question of whether the rule should be considered. Ryan characterized the health care legislation as "the mother of all unfunded mandates." Slaughter countered briefly by calling Ryan's point of order as "wasting time on parliamentary loopholes" aimed at "blocking much-needed health care reform in this nation." After several other members spoke on the point of order, the question of consideration (to proceed with debating and voting on the rule) was adopted, 228–195.[20]

Subsequently, another point of order was raised by Republican representative Darrell Issa of California that the special rule violated another House rule by waiving points of order against an earmark reporting requirement, triggering another twenty-minute debate with similar results.[21] After well over an hour spent on the rule, it was adopted at about 6 P.M., 224–206.

In closing debate for Republicans on the two measures, Republican leader John Boehner stated that the process and institution were broken, as a consequence producing a bill that is not what the American people need or want. The American people are frightened, disgusted, and angry, he said. He continued: "They're angry that no matter how they engage in this debate, this body moves forward against their will. Shame on us. Shame on this body. Shame on each and every one of you who substitutes your will and your desires above those of your fellow countrymen."[22]

In closing debate for the Democrats, Speaker Pelosi ignored Republican complaints about the process and instead emphasized the historic importance of passing health care reform as honoring the vows of the founders in the Declaration of Independence to secure the inalienable rights of life liberty and the pursuit of happiness: "This legislation will lead to healthier lives, more liberty to pursue hopes and dreams and happiness for the American people. This is an American proposal that honors the traditions of our country. Today we have the opportunity to complete the great unfinished business of our society and pass health insurance reform for all Americans. That is a right and not a privilege."[23]

The House adopted the motion to concur in the Senate amendments and then passed the reconciliation bill by similar near party-line votes of 219–212 and 220–211, respectively. Before that, a motion to recommit with instructions by Representative David Camp of Michigan to restore antiabortion language failed, 199–232. Thirty-four House Democrats voted against the Senate amendments, and 33 against the reconciliation bill. No Republicans voted for either measure.

The House had convened at 1 P.M. on Sunday, March 21, 2010, and completed its work shortly after midnight—debating and voting on the rule and the two health care measures (as well as a few noncontroversial measures under a suspension of the rules). After agreeing to the Senate amendments to the Affordable Care Act (HR 3590), the bill was sent to the president and signed into law on March 23.

The Senate, by contrast, would take another three days considering the health/education reconciliation bill (HR 4872), during which time forty-one Republican amendments were offered. The measure easily surmounted the 51-vote threshold for reconciliation, 56–43, with just 3 Democrats defecting and every Republican opposing.

The last minute discovery of minor Byrd rule violations forced those items to be dropped, thus requiring the revised bill to be returned to the House to be finally cleared for the president's signature. It passed, 220–207, on the evening of March 25, 2010.[24] President Obama signed the bill into law five-days later, on March 30, 2010.[25]

Concluding Thoughts

The saga of health care reform legislation in the 111th Congress is by now a familiar tale for major legislation in the contemporary Congress. With partisan polarization at its zenith and minority parties unwilling to cooperate or compromise with the majority on almost anything, especially with a president of the other party, it falls to the majority leadership to rely on extraordinary consultation, pressures, and compromises within its own ranks, as well as on a creative use of the rules, to eke out a victory on contentious legislation.

The health care effort could easily have failed without the concerted, ongoing efforts of the majority leadership in both houses and the president to corral wavering members and strike the appropriate deals. That the most vocal public was in opposition added to the uncertainty of the enterprise. It certainly contributed to the Republicans' retaking control of the House in the 2010 elections, which was aided by the weak economy and high jobless numbers. Boehner's final debate warning that public opposition to the legislation was not just partisan hyperbole was backed up six years after its enactment with most opinion polls still showed that a majority of the American people opposed to the law.[26]

Nevertheless, President Barack Obama was easily reelected in 2012. There is no question, though, that the Tea Party movement, ignited by the health care debate, figured prominently in Republicans' taking back the House in the 2010 elections and played some role in the Senate GOP's return to power in the 2014 midterm elections.

Perhaps in a 50/50 red-and-blue America, such electoral swings are inevitable—at least into the near future. The old conventional wisdom that bipartisan support is needed to pass and sustain support for major legislation may be just as true today as it once was. But in the meantime, parties still seem willing to take their chances on going it alone, as the Republican "repeal and replace" Obamacare debate, recounted in the final chapter of this book, reveals.

4

Fraying Purse Strings

SPEAKER JOHN BOEHNER'S RESIGNATION from the House in 2015 brought to a head internal disputes within the House GOP conference over how to deal with the federal budget. The revolt centered on the Freedom Caucus, a fiscally conservative group of members who are hard-liners when it comes to fiscal responsibility. The House had been beset for several years, under both parties, with difficulties in processing budget resolutions and spending bills, usually ending with continuing appropriations resolutions, and eventually omnibus money bills, often several months late.

The breakdown in what was once a bipartisan appropriations committee and spending process forced the majority party to engage in all manner of procedural contortions just to keep the government open (not always successfully, as the sixteen-day government shutdown in 2013 demonstrated). Majority party power plays are not always aimed at producing major legislative successes—especially in recent times—but at protecting the ruling party and its members from embarrassing failures that could lead to a loss of power at the next election. Increasingly, majority power plays are about simple survival in the highly charged culture of campaigning.

Speaker Boehner startled his Republican conference colleagues on the morning of September 25, 2015, by announcing that he was leaving the House at the end of October. As he explained to reporters afterward, "This turmoil that has been churning for a couple of months now is no good for the members. And it's not good for the institution."[1]

The turmoil was being churned by a forty-member faction of Boehner's own party known as the Freedom Caucus. It had turned against him, causing considerable internal strife in the conference. One Freedom Caucus member, Representative Mark Meadows of North Carolina, helped bring the revolt to a head by introducing a resolution in late July to remove Boehner as speaker.[2]

The resolution included a preamble consisting of eight "whereas" clauses, reminiscent of the "long train of abuses and usurpations" hurled against King George III in the Declaration of Independence. Boehner's offenses were notably less egregious than those of King George—they ranged from "inaction, that caused the power of Congress to atrophy"; to punishing members who did not vote the speaker's way; to using the Rules Committee "to limit meaningful amendments." The resolving clause read quite simply: "Resolved, That the office of Speaker is hereby declared to be vacant." The resolution was referred to the House Rules Committee where it languished over the next two months before becoming obsolete when Boehner stepped down.[3]

Although the resolution's list of grievances against Boehner was primarily procedural, it reflected a larger frustration among Freedom Caucus members that the speaker had failed, over his four and a half years in office, to deliver on Republicans' presumed mandate from the 2010 elections to reduce the size, scope, and costs of government and to repeal Obamacare. That agenda grew out of the electoral successes of the grassroots Tea Party

60

movement in 2010, which enabled Republicans to retake control of the House after four years of Democratic rule.

Notwithstanding Boehner's efforts to execute a high-wire act as party leader and constitutional officer, Congress went to the brink of a fiscal cliff in 2011 with a near default on the country's debt, which caused Standard & Poor to downgrade the nation's credit rating. In 2013, the GOP took the country over the cliff with a sixteen-day government shutdown in a futile attempt to leverage the operations of the government in return for repealing Obamacare.

In 2015, Congress faced the prospect of another government shutdown on October 1 and funding sequestration (across-the-board discretionary program cuts) as the two chambers and parties clashed over differing spending priorities. Included in that imbroglio was a Republican effort to defund Planned Parenthood over its alleged sale of fetal tissue. The government was operating under stringent statutory spending caps occasioned by the 2011 collapse of negotiations to achieve a "grand bargain" on the budget with the White House. Failure to live within the statutory caps would result in a mandatory sequestration order implementing spending cuts to achieve compliance.

Ironically, it was Obama's Office of Management and Budget and legislative affairs directors, Jack Lew and Rob Nabors, who had proposed using the sequestration process as an action-forcing mechanism to produce a budget compromise in 2011. It was based on the premise that Republicans would never allow the trigger to be pulled given the drastic cuts it would cause in defense spending. Congress went along with the Lew-Nabors proposal but still did not reach an alternative budget deal agreement.[4] Consequently, when the budget talks collapsed, the sequester axe fell, leaving all sides reeling.

Two days after Boehner announced his resignation to his GOP colleagues in September, he appeared on CBS's *Face the Nation* and confidently predicted that Congress would pass a continuing resolution before October 1, avoiding a government shutdown. The speaker said he would continue to help pass conservative legislation during his last month in office, adding: "I don't want to leave my successor a dirty barn. I want to clean the barn up a little bit before the next person gets there."[5]

Cleaning Up the Barn

Boehner's vision for "cleaning up the barn" was breaking the fiscal impasse over appropriations and averting another debt limit crisis. In this way, he could leave his successor some running room for the fiscal year ahead. Given the short time frame remaining, setting things right would entail working behind the scenes with his GOP leadership allies, Democratic leaders, and the Obama White House.

Boehner made good on his first prediction, passing a continuing appropriations bill to keep the government operating through December 11 and also defunded Planned Parenthood. The Senate stripped the Planned Parenthood provision and sent the measure back to the House, which cleared the bill for the president on fiscal New Year's Eve (September 30) by a bipartisan vote of 277–151, with 91 Republicans voting in favor and 151 voting against.

Boehner then began the barn cleaning in earnest, with an eye to reconciling spending differences and preventing a debt default. High-level negotiations proceeded behind closed doors between House and Senate leadership staff members and the White House. The resulting deal, cleared for the president in the wee hours of October 30, 2015, raised existing spending caps by $80 billion—roughly $50 billion in fiscal year 2016 and $30 billion in 2017, divided equally between defense and nondefense spending.

It was the second time in two years that Congress loosened the stringent caps established by the Budget Control Act of 2011. The act called for some $900 billion in deficit reductions between

2012 and 2021. The heavy hit on both domestic and defense spending from the 2011 legislation gave incentive for Democrats and Republicans alike to find common ground in 2013 and 2015. Both agreements included small cuts in entitlements—savings in 2013 from student loans, federal retirement, and other programs, and in 2015 from changes in Medicare and Social Security.

The 2015 bill also suspended the debt limit until March 15, 2017. It was Boehner's final gift, and it cleared the House on October 28, the same day Representative Paul Ryan (R-WI) was nominated speaker by the GOP conference. In selling the package to his Republican colleagues, Boehner claimed the spending ceilings were still lower than the presequester ceilings from 2011—$1.067 trillion in base discretionary spending in fiscal year 2016, compared with $1.107 trillion in the presequester law caps.[6] When the Congressional Budget Office released an estimate shortly before House consideration that showed the package still spent more than it saved, fiscal conservatives were furious. Initial leadership panic was followed quickly by last-minute legerdemain in a special rule reported by the House Rules Committee—the "speaker's committee."[7]

The budget package was tacked onto a previously House- and Senate-passed bill (HR 1314) that had originally provided tax exempt organizations a right to appeal their status. The advantage of such bait-and-switch tactics is to avoid the more prolonged process in both chambers necessitated by introducing an entirely new bill. Shortly after the package was posted online, speaker-designate Ryan was asked by a CNN interviewer what he thought of it. Though he had not yet read it, he replied—perhaps as a rhetorical sop to his Freedom Caucus colleagues—"This process stinks." He promised that "under new management, we're not going to do business like this," suggesting that the Republican conference "should have been meeting months ago to develop a strategy on this."[8] Nevertheless, he came around to supporting and voting for the deal.

The special rule from the Rules Committee substituted the language from the budget agreement for the tax exempt organizations' appeal language, along with a new title, the "Bipartisan Budget Act of 2015." It passed the House, 266–167, with all 187 Democrats voting in favor, along with 79 of the 246 Republicans who voted. The following day, October 29, the Senate followed suit, 64–35, with 18 Republicans and all 44 Democrats voting in favor, and 35 Republicans voting against.[9]

Ryan's Reign

In his acceptance speech as speaker on October 29, 2015, Ryan readily conceded that "the House is broken"; committees need "to retake the lead in drafting all major legislation"; and the process should be opened to all members, including the minority." In summary, he said, "we need to return to regular order."[10]

In June 2016, Ryan fulfilled a promise to his GOP colleagues to develop from the bottom up an agenda to change the way the House manages the nation's business. The final product, labeled "A Better Way: Our Vision for a Confident America," was a forward-looking agenda for the country covering the areas of poverty, national security, the economy, the Constitution, health care, and tax reform. The plan was developed under the aegis of the Republican conference and the GOP Policy Committee, respectively, chaired by representatives Cathy McMorris Rodgers of Washington and Luke Messer of Indiana. Ryan, a longtime policy wonk, was in a strong position to shepherd the effort.

The "Constitution" section of the agenda included a damning indictment of Congress's stewardship of the purse strings that could well be an epigraph to this chapter: "The people granted Congress the power to write laws, raise revenues, and spend and borrow money on behalf of the United States. There is no power more consequential. . . . Yet for decades, Congress has let this power atrophy—thereby depriving the people of their voice."[11]

In the subsection "Exercise Power of the Purse," the agenda called for a return to passing annual appropriations bills and removing Senate impediments to doing so (specifically referring to the sixty-vote cloture threshold for ending filibusters against taking up money bills). It advocated overhauling the outdated and needlessly complex Congressional Budget Act; required committees of jurisdiction to conduct comprehensive reviews of all spending not subject to annual appropriations; and promoted "the strategic use of limitations, funding conditionality, and funding availability to make congressional action in appropriations bills more effective."[12]

The new speaker's commitment to restoring regular order in the House enabled the House to come together in a bipartisan agreement before Christmas in 2015 to complete action on the fiscal 2016 appropriations process. Speaker Boehner's parting gift of a clean barn—a fiscal framework for completing action on the fiscal 2016 appropriations bills by the end of 2015—made it easier to complete the process in December 2015. However, it took three continuing resolutions in December to avoid the dreaded government shutdown before a final, consolidated appropriations bill was agreed to by both chambers and signed into law by President Obama.[13]

Senate Majority Leader Mitch McConnell, wrapping up his first year as leader of the upper house, declared, "By any objective standard, I think, the Senate is back to work." Newly minted House Speaker Ryan similarly boasted, "We passed more major legislation in a few weeks than we have in a few years," pointing to enactment of major education, highway, and tax-cut legislation in addition to the consolidated money bill. Although the Republicans had to drop their push in the omnibus bill for defunding Planned Parenthood and barring Iraqi and Syrian refugees, they could take solace in ending a forty-year ban on crude oil exports.[14]

As Congress entered 2016 and began work on the fiscal 2017 budget process, it quickly slid back into its slapdash ways of division and delays. In a January 2017 column, I summarized this recurring pattern of congressional dysfunction as follows: "The House again becomes entangled in the chaos of authorization logjams, policy-laden appropriations bills, lack of Senate responsiveness to House initiatives, and lack of conference committees to resolve differences between the two bodies. Budget deadlines are missed, [and] money bills wither on the vine, unpicked. It all inevitably leads to a last-minute crush to cram everything into unread, omnibus legislation as the express ticket out of town—one step ahead of the law (whatever might be in it)."[15]

Briefly, here is how fiscal 2017 unfolded. The House Budget Committee reported its budget resolution on March 23, 2016. But the Freedom Caucus put up strong resistance to the spending levels, and the resolution was abandoned and never brought to the floor. It was only the second time since the Budget Act's 1974 enactment that the House Budget Committee failed to bring its budget resolution to a vote in the House. Meanwhile, the Senate Budget Committee did not even try to report a resolution on grounds that the 2015 bipartisan budget agreement would suffice—although it lacked the requisite numbers for debt and deficit.

The House Appropriations Committee offered its usual diligence in reporting all twelve of its appropriations bills by July 22. Yet the committee only managed to pass six of its bills through the House before pulling the plug on the process in mid-July, presumably due to the Senate's inability to bring up any of the appropriations bills. A continuing appropriations resolution was enacted on September 28, 2016, continuing the operations of government through December 9. It consisted of an amendment to the House-passed Legislative Branch Appropriations bill but was titled the "Continuing Appropriations and Military Construction,

Veterans Affairs, and Related Agencies Appropriations Act, 2017, and Zika Response and Preparedness Act."

Although it was anticipated that Congress would complete action on a wrap-up omnibus bill for the remaining eleven regular bills in December, as it had in 2015, the surprising election of Republican Donald Trump as president threw a cog in the wheel. With the prospect of unified party government for the first time since 2010 (when President Obama last had a Democratic House and Senate), Republicans deferred to the new president-elect's wishes to offer his own budget priorities for the remainder of fiscal 2017. And so the can was kicked further down the road with another continuing resolution—this one through April 28, 2017.

Further complicating the fiscal 2017 picture was a decision to belatedly bring up a budget resolution in January 2017 to enable a reconciliation bill supporting the repeal of Obamacare—the Republican-loathed health care plan. A similar maneuver, using reconciliation, failed in 2015 when President Obama vetoed the repeal bill and Congress did not have the two-thirds votes to override his veto. This time, both houses dutifully passed the delinquent budget resolution in early January 2017, once again setting the process in motion. Yet the stakes were much higher with the Republicans controlling both branches and therefore accountable for crafting an acceptable replacement for Obamacare. (For more on this, see chapter 7.)

The unusual prolonging of the fiscal 2017 budget process was bound to cause problems. With 2017 funding still unsettled, fiscal year 2018 loomed quickly. The president's fiscal 2018 budget was theoretically due the first Monday in February (two weeks after his inauguration), although Congress traditionally cuts new presidents slack on this deadline. The final fiscal 2018 congressional budget resolution is still supposed to be completed by April 15, and this would presumably include instructions for another reconciliation bill, this one dealing with tax reform.

A Doubtful Pledge in a New Era

In being sworn in as speaker at the beginning of the 115th Congress on January 3, 2017, Speaker Paul Ryan again pledged "to restore regular order, get the committee system working again, [and] hold regular House and Senate conferences, because only a fully functioning House can really, truly do the people's business."[16]

However, it was clear from the outset that legislative overload produced by a new administration, armed with its perceived electoral mandate, would force Congress to circumvent the regular order on a regular basis to keep up. This was evident in January 2017, when both the Senate and House adopted an unreported budget resolution to facilitate reconciliation on Obamacare (the House even shut out the usual round of substitute budget amendments by various factions, including the minority party).

How Did This Happen?

The fiscal contortions of the Republican-controlled 114th Congress related here are not meant as an indictment of a single party. These patterns have been recurring over the course of recent Congresses under both Democrats and Republicans. Factually, the history of congressional control of the country's purse strings has always been tenuous, and in modern times is traceable at least back to the 1970s when mounting budget deficits forced Congress to enact the Congressional Budget and Impoundment Control Act of 1974. The act was intended to produce more centralized and coordinated control of spending priorities, deficits, debt, and revenues—independent of executive control.

However, the Budget Act proved no panacea for curing out-of-control spending. Instead, the history of congressional budgeting in recent decades has been marked by periodic crises, confrontations, and, ultimately, conciliation and compromise brokered by commissions, special "super" committees, or high-level, inter-branch budget summits.

A brief survey of the budget and appropriations record in Congress reveals just how badly the process has deteriorated. Over the forty-one-year history of the Congressional Budget Act (fiscal years 1976–2017), Congress has failed on ten occasions to adopt a final budget resolution (legally required by mid-April) even before the October 1 start of the fiscal year. All but one of those instances occurred in this new century (the other was in fiscal 1999). The House has a much better track record than the Senate, failing on only two occasions to adopt its own budget resolution before October 1 (in fiscal years 2011 and 2017).[17]

On appropriations bills, Congress's track record has also been abysmal: on only four occasions since the Budget Act took full effect has Congress enacted all the regular appropriations bills before the start of the fiscal year—in fiscal years 1977, 1989, 1995, and 1997—even though the Budget Act moved the start of the fiscal year from July 1 to October 1.

Congress's tardiness in completing its work has gotten progressively worse. In ten of the last twenty fiscal years, 1998 through 2017, Congress has not enacted any of the regular appropriations bills on time. On seven of these occasions, the final congressional wrap-up of the appropriations process spilled over into the following calendar year, including fiscal 2017.[18] Budget crises are human-made political phenomena occurring when Congress runs up against a known budgetary deadline—whether over expiring appropriations for the operation of government, the need to increase the debt ceiling, or both. The imperative to keep the government boat afloat with "must-pass" bills becomes an inducement for parties to bring on board their extraneous partisan baggage as well.

The recurring budgetary challenges have brought Congress and the nation to the brink so often that, in recent years, these crisis points have come to be known as "fiscal cliffs." Reaching the edge usually involves more than a game of numbers. In the background, and often foreground, of budgetary roulette are serious policy differences—the most obvious examples in recent years being clashes over Obamacare and Planned Parenthood. But numerous other differences with an administration of another party have prompted these mini- and maxi-crises. Let's look at some examples of how the Republicans approached their policy and budgetary responsibilities when they retook control of the House in 2011 after four years under a Democratic majority.

A New Beginning

Even before the 112th Congress convened in January 2011, the Tea Party influence on the revitalized Republican Party was evident. On September 23, 2010, House Republican leaders rolled out their Pledge to America at a hardware store in Sterling, Virginia. This pledge was reminiscent of the Newt Gingrich–led Contract with America in 1994, but without the hoopla of a signing ceremony on the Capitol steps. The five-plank pledge committed House Republicans to implementing plans to create jobs and end economic uncertainty; stop out-of-control spending and reduce the size of government; repeal and replace the government takeover of health care; reform Congress and restore trust; keep the nation secure at home and abroad; and restore the constitutional system of checks and balances.[19]

The opening day of the 112th Congress, on January 6, 2011, was a celebration of that victory and commitment, beginning with Ohio representative John Boehner's election and acceptance speech as speaker. He promised to "honor our pledge to America, . . . stand firm on our constitutional principles, . . . [and] do these things in a manner that restores and respects the time-honored right of the minority to an honest debate and a fair, open process."[20] This spirit continued in the adoption of changes in

House rules from the previous Congress. On budget-related matters, the new rules made a bow to reducing spending and cutting government, at least symbolically. Among the budget-related rules changes were provisions to require that committee oversight plans include proposals to eliminate duplicative government programs; allow members to direct that savings from their cutting amendments to appropriations bills be directed to a "spending reduction account"; and repeal the so-called Gephardt rule that provided for spinning off the debt limit number from a concurrent budget resolution into a joint resolution and deeming it automatically passed by the House, without a separate vote.[21]

Another budget-related provision replaced the "pay-as-you-go" (PAYGO) budgeting rules with a "cut-as-you-go" (CUTGO) rule. The former rule, initially adopted as part of the 1990 Budget Enforcement Act, and then enshrined in rules and law by the Democratic majority in 2007, required that any measure increasing entitlement benefits or reducing revenues be offset with equivalent amounts of entitlement cuts and/or tax increases. The new CUTGO rule, conversely, confined the offset requirement to entitlement increases and did not require that tax cuts be paid for. Moreover, the new rule expressly prohibited using tax increases to offset entitlement benefit increases.

During debate on the rules package, the PAYGO let-go became a central focus. Ranking House Budget Committee member Democrat Chris Van Hollen (MD) observed that the Republicans had spent months on the campaign trail "telling the American people they wanted to reduce deficits and debt, [but] this rule opens the door to larger deficits and a bigger national debt."[22] Budget Committee chairman Paul Ryan (R-WI), the future speaker, rebutted Van Hollen: "After the last two Congresses, PAYGO was gimmicked or waived 32 times, to the net total of $932 billion in extra deficit spending. But when PAYGO was used, when it was invoked, it was more often used to raises taxes."[23] The new rules also gave the Budget Committee chairman authority to establish suballocations for the appropriations subcommittees if a budget resolution was not in place, and it made those ceilings binding for the twelve appropriations measures once floor action was completed on each.[24]

The House predictably adopted the GOP rules package for the 112th Congress along party lines, setting the table to move quickly on the Republican agenda. Not a day was lost. On the second day of the 112th Congress, the House began work to repeal Obamacare—establishing a pattern for dozens of votes over the next five years to repeal the health care law in whole or in part; however, the House-passed legislation inevitably died in the Democratic-controlled Senate.

The Omnibus Amendment Bill

The next major budget-related bill Congress dealt with was the "Full-Year Continuing Appropriations Act, 2011," designed to finish the fiscal year 2011 appropriations process left over from the previous Congress. Such a calendar year bump-over for completing appropriations was becoming a recurring pattern. None of the twelve regular money bills had been enacted into law by the beginning of the fiscal year—October 1, 2010—and the continuing resolution enacted at the end of the previous Congress only funded the government through March 4, 2011.

Boehner exercised his prerogative to designate the full-year spending bill as HR 1.[25] On February 11, the full text of HR 1 was introduced by Appropriations Committee chairman Hal Rogers of Kentucky and referred to the Appropriations and Budget committees—there was no expectation that either committee would act on the bill. Instead, the leadership sent the measure to the House Rules Committee for a special rule that implicitly discharged the two committees from further consideration.

The Rules Committee reported a modified, open amendment rule on February 14 (H. Res. 92) that allowed for the offering of any amendment provided it complied with House rules and was filed in the *Congressional Record* at least one day before its consideration.[26] Boehner was trying to make good on two of the GOP pledge promises—a more open floor amendment process and opportunities to reduce government spending. As with most special rules, the rule was reported on a party-line vote and adopted by the House the next day, again along party lines. What ensued was a veritable amendment free-for-all over the next four days. More than 580 amendments were filed in the *Congressional Record*, although only 126 were ultimately offered and voted on. All told, 66 amendments were adopted and 60 were rejected; the Republicans were successful on 55 of their amendments, and Democrats were successful on 11 of theirs.

More than half the amendments considered (54 percent) were so-called limitation amendments because they prohibited agencies from using any of their funds on specified activities. Of these, 45 were adopted and 23 were rejected. Ten of the limitation amendments, all by Republicans and all adopted, defunded parts of Obamacare. Another 14 Republican limitation amendments adopted barred some aspects of agency activity on environmental regulations or projects, or climate change.[27]

An example of a limitation amendment is Amendment No. 404, successfully offered by Representative Greg Walden (R-OR) to HR 1, to block the Federal Communication Commission's "network neutrality rules." It reads as follows: "None of the funds made available by this Act may be used to implement the Report and Order of the Federal Communications Commission relating to the matter of preserving the open Internet and broadband industry practices (FCC 10–201, adopted by the Commission on December 21, 2010)."[28] Limitation amendments were obviously more popular than amendments that reduce spending (which accounted for only a third of the total amendments considered). For one thing, twice as many limitation amendments succeeded as failed, whereas twice as many spending reduction amendments failed as succeeded.

This was also the case during consideration of individual appropriations bills, which were previously considered under mostly open amendment rules.[29] For example, in examining the amendment process on the seven appropriations bills considered by the House in 2012 (for fiscal year 2013), I identified 42 percent of the amendments as limitation amendments, followed by off-setting amendments at 29 percent, and cutting amendments at 24 percent.

On February 18, 2011, the omnibus bill finally passed 235–189, with just 3 Republicans voting "nay" and no Democrats voting "aye." The measure was loaded with so many policy-related limitation amendments that it predictably sank under its own weight in the Democrat-controlled Senate. On March 4, Senate Appropriations Committee chairman Daniel K. Inouye (D-HI) attempted to pass a Democratic substitute amendment, but it fell 18 votes short of the 60 needed under a unanimous consent agreement. Congress would eventually settle on a pared down compromise in mid-April after two more continuing resolutions.

Reflecting in 2015 on Speaker Boehner's 2011 inaugural flight with an open amendment process on the wrap-up money bill (HR 1), Boehner's good friend and Ohio colleague, Representative Steve LaTourette, wrote that "John's reward [for the open rule] was to be treated to one of the most bizarre legislative exercises any of us in the House could remember." LaTourette, who retired at the end of the 112th Congress (and died in 2016), said that he and his friends expected the Democrats "to exploit the opportunity to stall the bill." But "it was the far right-wing Republicans, ushered in by the 2010 Tea Party wave, who filed hundreds of amendments to attack a bill" that had been drafted by their own party's leaders. By giving members more freedom and opportunity, Boehner believed they would rally around the party's overall goals. "Boy, was he wrong!" LaTourette exclaimed. "His steady temperament and desire to treat every member with respect and friendship was repaid with plots and palace intrigue—an internal rebellion that would span his speakership and intensify as time went on."[30]

Conclusions

When former House Appropriations Committee staff director Jim Dyer was asked in 2013 about the "decline of the cardinals"—the chairs of the twelve appropriations subcommittees—he replied, "What has happened to the cardinals is what happened to the [other] committees." And, he elaborated, "people say appropriations are broken and dead. Well, my response to that is, authorizers are broken and dead. The budget is broken and dead too. Tell me what isn't broken and dead."[31]

Nothing that has happened since Dyer's dire dirge has resurrected Congress. Paul Ryan's first remarks as speaker in October 2015 simply confirmed the obvious: "The House is broken." Ryan had been witnessing the continuing breakdown since entering the House in 1999. Moreover, he had been at the fiscal vortex of its fraying purse strings as chairman of both the Budget and Ways and Means committees during the five years preceding his election as speaker.

Increasing partisan polarization over the last quarter century has been a major contributor to budgetary deadlocks, crises, and cliffs. The chasm has not only widened between the parties and the White House but often inside the ruling party's own ranks. Leaders of both parties, when in the majority, use what little leverage they have to hold their parties and chambers together, even if it requires using innovative procedural devices at the expense of the minority party and often of individual members of their own party. The transparency in Congress (driving more major decisions behind closed doors), the increasing independence of members, and the ever-present threat of losing individual seats and party control of either house all militate against leaders using more coercive tactics on their own colleagues even as opportunities for individual member input decline.

Leadership in Congress is an intricate balancing act, difficult to sustain for extended periods, as former Speaker John Boehner learned the hard way. In his first full year as speaker, Paul Ryan ran up against those same harsh realities, failing to adopt a budget resolution or separately enact any of the regular appropriations bills. The challenge for any speaker is to learn from the successes and failures of his or her predecessors in hopes that over the long haul a modicum of regular order and fiscal sobriety can be restored.

5

Whither the War Power?

IF THERE IS A TERM that captures Congress's attitude toward presidents' exercise of war powers, it might be "benign ambivalence." Unlike "benign neglect" (a term torn from an unrelated leaked memo during Richard Nixon's presidency), benign ambivalence reflects the varying degrees of congressional involvement in and support for presidential commitments of military force to foreign hostilities.[1] It is benign because it is usually well intentioned, although not necessarily responsive or responsible. Implicit in this description is the notion that presidents tend to initiate military interventions and Congress reacts to them, one way or another. It flies in the face of the constitutional charge that Congress shall have the sole power to declare war. How and why this role reversal has occurred parallels the discussion of Congress's frayed purse strings in the previous chapter.

Congressional party leaders enable and facilitate benign ambivalence about committing to foreign interventions by protecting members from direct votes on a military commitment that could come back to bite them in the next election, or at least provide them a vote on a nonbinding alternative. Part of the culture of campaigning is avoiding accountability for potential disasters by deferring to—or questioning—the president's initial decision to intervene in overseas hostilities while still providing the necessary funds "in support of our troops." The case studies on Libya, Syria, and the rise of the Islamic State of Iraq and Syria globally during the Obama presidency show how congressional leaders finesse this conundrum by feigning involvement and concern while keeping their members away from the politically harmful crossfire.

In the Beginning

In a 1798 letter to Thomas Jefferson, reacting to President John Adams's waging a quasi-war against France, James Madison explains succinctly why the founders lodged the war power in Congress: "The Constitution supposes, what the history of all governments demonstrates, that the Executive is the branch of power most interested in war and most prone to it. It has accordingly, with studied care, vested the question of war in the Legislative."[2]

Yet the last time Congress declared war was at the outset of World War II when declarations were voted against six Axis powers. Since then, when Congress has approved military actions abroad, it has relied on what are known today as authorizations for the use of military force (AUMF). Two Supreme Court rulings at the turn of the nineteenth century involving America's quasi-war with France held that such statutes are equivalent to declarations of war.[3]

Ironically, in the first major conflict after World War II, the Korean War, President Harry Truman did not ask Congress for either a declaration of war or an AUMF. Nor did Congress press him to request such authority (although it could have acted unilaterally). Because North Korea's invasion of South Korea in 1950 was a violation of state sovereignty and of the United Nations

Charter, the UN Security Council adopted a resolution ordering North Korea to withdraw. Truman used the resolution as justification for deploying American troops to repel the invasion—even before another UN resolution was adopted approving a military response. Truman characterized America's intervention as a UN "police action" and not a war.

Congress's reaction was largely passive, even though Truman's actions violated special agreements enshrined in the UN Participation Act of 1945 that require congressional approval of any military action taken by the president. Truman's unilateral initiative established a precedent on which subsequent presidents (George H. W. Bush, Bill Clinton, and Barack Obama) would rely.[4]

The Vietnam Quagmire

On August 4, 1964, President Lyndon Johnson reported in a televised address that North Vietnamese torpedo boats had attacked the American destroyer *Maddox* in the Gulf of Tonkin off Vietnam. Although the US destroyer was not hit, Johnson ordered a retaliatory response and called on congressional leaders to adopt a resolution making clear US determination to take all steps necessary in support of freedom and peace in Southeast Asia. Congress responded quickly, and the Senate passed the so-called Tonkin Gulf Resolution on August 6, with only two dissenting votes. The House followed suit by a unanimous vote the following day.[5]

The operative language of the resolution stated that Congress "approves and supports the determination of the President, as Commander in Chief, to take all necessary measures to repel any armed attack against the forces of the United States and to prevent further aggression." The resolution goes on to commit the United States, "as the President determines, to take all necessary steps, including the use of armed force," to assist any member of the Southeast Asia Collective Defense Treaty "requesting assistance in defense of its freedom." Finally, the grant of authority was resolved to expire when the president determines that "the peace and security of the area is reasonably assured," or earlier if Congress terminates the authority by adopting a concurrent resolution.[6]

The resolution, framed as promoting "peace and security in southeast Asia," became Johnson's blank check to prosecute a prolonged war against North Vietnam and the Viet Cong guerillas in the south. Shortly after the 1964 presidential election, Johnson began escalating America's troop presence in South Vietnam from a few thousand advisers to what would eventually total more than 500,000 combat troops.

It was not until 1972, under President Richard Nixon, that a peace agreement was struck between North Vietnam and South Vietnam and the United States, paving the way for American withdrawal. As Nixon was drawing down troop levels in 1970, he ordered the invasion of Cambodia and Laos to clean out North Vietnamese sanctuaries. This broadening of the war into other countries ignited a national protest across the nation and on Capitol Hill, including a protest rally at Kent State University in Ohio at which four students were killed by National Guard troops. The outcry over the perceived widening of the war set in motion the wheels that eventually led to enactment of the War Powers Resolution of 1973, over President Nixon's veto.

The War Powers Resolution

The War Powers Resolution recognizes that the constitutional powers of the president as commander in chief to introduce US forces into hostilities or theaters where imminent hostilities are indicated can only be exercised pursuant to a declaration of war, a specific statutory authorization, or a national emergency created by an attack on the United States, its territories or possessions, or its armed forces.

At the same time, the final House-Senate war powers compromise took on a schizophrenic character by allowing presidents to commit troops to imminent or actual hostilities without the prior approval of Congress, or in response to a direct attack on the United States, as long as a sixty-day time limit on the deployment is observed (subject to a thirty-day extension by Congress, or if deemed necessary by the president, to ensure a safe withdrawal process).

Moreover, the law requires that, in every possible instance, before committing US troops to actual or imminent hostilities, the president must consult with Congress in advance and then report to it within forty-eight hours after the deployment on the circumstances necessitating the commitment, the authority for doing so, and the estimated scope and duration of the commitment. Finally, the president is required to report to Congress periodically thereafter, at least once every six months.[7]

Although President Nixon said he agreed with Congress's desire to assert its proper role in the conduct of foreign affairs, in his veto message he stated that "the restrictions which this resolution would impose are both unconstitutional and dangerous to the best interests of our Nation." Absent an extension by Congress, the resolution would automatically cut off, after sixty days, certain authorities that Nixon said have been exercised by presidents for more than two hundred years. He also singled out the resolution's granting Congress unilateral authority to force an earlier termination of a deployment by concurrent resolution, without the president's approval. Moreover, Nixon said the resolution undermines the ability of the United States to act decisively in times of international crisis.

Perhaps the most prescient observation of Nixon's veto message was his charge that the resolution "would give every future Congress the ability to handcuff every future President merely by doing nothing and sitting still. One cannot be a responsible partner," he concluded, "unless one is prepared to take responsible action."[8] Notwithstanding Nixon's objections, Congress enacted the legislation over his veto.

The track record of presidents and Congress since enactment of the War Powers Resolution has been mixed at best. Contrary to popular myth, not every president has agreed with Nixon that the War Powers Resolution is unconstitutional, although most have equivocated at times over exactly what specific actions trigger its coverage.[9] But like Nixon, most have given at least lip service to the consultation and periodic reporting requirements.

Since enactment of the War Powers Resolution in 1973, there have been four uses of military force authorizations: Lebanon, in 1982; the Gulf War against Iraq, in 1991; the war on terrorism, in 2001; and the invasion of Iraq, in 2002. Moreover, since enactment of the War Powers Resolution, the United States has been involved in at least eight military engagements not authorized by Congress, including Grenada in 1982, the Libyan air campaign in 2011, and the war on the Islamic State of Iraq and Syria (ISIS), beginning in 2014, depending on how broadly one interprets the 2001 AUMF against those responsible for September 11, 2001.[10]

The Ambivalence Conundrum

Congress's response to new military challenges over the eight years of the Obama presidency, similar to that under previous presidents, attests to its posture of benign ambivalence—waxing hot and cold, interested and disinterested, indignant and deferential. Two theories explain Congress's ambivalence toward its war powers responsibilities, and they are not necessarily mutually exclusive. One is that Congress has lost a strong "institutional identity" on foreign affairs and national security policy by not pursuing concerted oversight of the executive.[11]

A somewhat contrarian thesis explaining congressional ambivalence toward foreign affairs and war powers' responsibilities is that "the dearth of congressional oversight between 2000 and 2006 is nothing new"; that "good old-fashioned partisan politics has been, and continues to be, at play"; and that "the partisan composition of Congress has historically been the decisive factor in determining whether lawmakers will oppose or acquiesce in presidential calls for war."[12]

The Obama Presidency

In a December 2007 *Boston Globe* survey of presidential candidates on executive power issues, the nine candidates were asked under what circumstances the president would have constitutional authority to bomb Iran without seeking an AUMF from Congress. Illinois Democratic senator Barack Obama responded: "The President does not have power under the Constitution to unilaterally authorize a military attack in a situation that does not involve stopping an actual or imminent threat to the nation." He went on to say that a president has constitutional authority to act in self-defense without first seeking consent from Congress but that "history has shown us time and again . . . that military action is most successful when it is authorized and supported by the Legislative branch."[13]

Obama went on to win the Democratic nomination for the presidency in 2008 by besting New York senator Hillary Rodham Clinton. His early opposition to the Iraq war as an Illinois state senator, contrasted with Clinton's support for the 2002 Iraq AUMF in the US Senate, carried considerable weight with the antiwar sentiment prevalent in the Democratic base—a sentiment dating back to the Vietnam War protest days.

Obama did make clear during the campaign, however, that he was not an antiwar candidate. He vowed that as president he would quickly extricate the United States from what he considered to be the wrong war in Iraq, but he pledged to focus his efforts on winning what he considered the right war in Afghanistan against those responsible for the 9/11 terrorist attacks on the United States.

The remainder of this chapter looks at how well President Barack Obama abided by the views he expressed in the 2007 survey on the limits of presidential war powers, examining the new challenges posed by Libya, Syria's use of chemical weapons against its own people, and the rise of ISIS across the Middle East and elsewhere. In each new action, Obama's 2007 quotation about the need for congressional authority would not only be thrown back at him by his critics but by himself as he agonized in internal White House deliberations over the right course of action. Those deliberations, in turn, spilled over into congressional and public debates in an already war-weary nation.

Libya

On February 17, 2011, encouraged by the "Arab Spring" that was convulsing Tunisia and Egypt, protests broke out in Libya against the dictatorial regime of Colonel Muammar el-Qaddafi. When the protests escalated into open rebellion, Qaddafi responded by ordering his troops to attack, reportedly killing hundreds in Benghazi alone. He vowed to hunt down the rebels "door to door" and "show no mercy."

On March 17, 2011, the United Nations Security Council passed a resolution introduced by France to enforce a no-fly zone over Libya to protect protesters from massacre. The Obama administration was initially ambivalent about the wisdom of the resolution but eventually signed on, assisted in its passage, and agreed to participate in its implementation by flying sorties with its NATO allies.

Although the initial criticism emanating from some in Congress was that the president was indecisive about supporting the French initiative, once the president did commit, the criticism shifted to blaming the president for failure to consult with Congress in advance, and for not seeking congressional approval for US participation in the air campaign. I described Congress's ambivalence over exercising its war powers at the time of the Libyan intervention this way: "Its war dance is often a salsa sidestep—four steps left, four steps right, and lots of swaying back and forth." This is especially evident "absent a presidential request to use force or overwhelming public sentiment for or against military action. Members prefer avoiding political risks when military failure is a possibility."[14]

An early example of this tepid congressional approach regarding Libya occurred on March 1, 2011, when Democratic senator Chuck Schumer of New York called up a resolution on the Senate floor that "strongly condemn[ed] the gross and systematic violations of human rights in Libya, including violent attacks on protesters demanding democratic reforms." The resolution, introduced by Democratic senator Robert Menendez of New Jersey and cosponsored by ten other senators, was called up by Schumer (one of the cosponsors) on the same day it was introduced. The "sense of the Senate" resolution commended the brave protesters; condemned the violent attacks on protesters; called on Qaddafi to resign; welcomed the UN Security Council vote to refer the matter to the International Criminal Court and urged it to take further steps, "including the possible imposition of a no-fly zone"; welcomed the US government outreach to Libyan opposition figures; and supported "an orderly, irreversible transition to a legitimate democratic government in Libya."[15]

Although Senate passage of the resolution was later hailed by one House member as an overwhelming, unanimous vote, the fact is the resolution was passed by unanimous consent, without debate, a vote, or even statements of support inserted in the *Congressional Record*. Nonetheless, the Senate was on record as being outraged by the violence against innocent civilians in Libya (whether most senators knew it or not).

To his credit, Obama convened a bipartisan congressional leadership meeting at the White House the day after the March 17 UN vote. Members still complained this was not the kind of advance consultation contemplated by the War Powers Resolution and objected to being presented with a done deal. The president did comply with the War Powers Resolution's forty-eight-hour reporting requirement, notifying Congress by letter March 21 on "the commencement of operations." The timing of this activity could not have been worse (or perhaps better, from the administration's standpoint), as Congress left town on March 18 for a ten-day recess and the president flew off shortly thereafter on a five-day Latin American tour.

In his March 21 letter, the president indicated that the mission authorized by the UN Security Council, and undertaken with the support of European allies and Arab partners, was "to prevent a humanitarian catastrophe and address the threat posed to international peace and security by the crisis in Libya." As to the US interest, the president said that, "left unaddressed, the growing instability in Libya could ignite wider instability in the Middle East, with dangerous consequences to the national security interests of the United States." Finally, the president emphasized that the United States "has not deployed ground forces into Libya," and that it is "conducting a limited and well-defined mission . . . to protect civilians and prevent a humanitarian disaster."[16]

The letter's justifications for US involvement only raised more questions. On March 23, House Speaker John Boehner sent the president a two-page letter indicating that he and his colleagues "are troubled that US military resources were committed to war without clearly defining for the American people, the Congress and our troops what the mission in Libya is and what America's role is in achieving that mission." The letter went on to raise a host of specific questions. When it became apparent that the controversy would not fade over the congressional recess, the president cut his Latin American tour short and returned to Washington to mend fences.

On March 28, the Senate's first day back in town, Senate Republican leader Mitch McConnell used his morning hour floor speech to pose further questions he said he hoped the president would address in his nationally televised speech that evening: "When will the US combat role in the operation end? Will America's commitment end in days, not weeks, as the president promised? What will be the duration of the noncombat operation, and what will be the cost? What national security interests of the United States justify the risk of American life? What is the role of our country in Libya's ongoing civil war?"[17]

In his televised address that evening, delivered at the National Defense University, the president traced the background of US support for a UN-sanctioned no-fly zone over Libya to protect innocent civilians from being massacred. "Qaddafi declared he would show 'no mercy' to his own people," Obama said. "He compared them to rats, and threatened to go door to door to inflict punishment. . . . If we waited one more day, Benghazi . . . could suffer a massacre that would have reverberated across the region and stained the conscience of the world. It was not in our national interest to let that happen."

The president reiterated that the US role was limited, "that we would not put ground troops into Libya." The bulk of the operation had already been turned over to NATO, he said. And he made clear, despite the urging of some to bring down Qaddafi, that "broadening our military mission to include regime change would be a mistake." Such an action would splinter the coalition and would likely involve putting US troops on the ground. "To be blunt, we went down that road in Iraq. . . . That is not something we can afford to repeat in Libya."[18]

Notwithstanding the president's characterization of the US role as narrowing to a "supporting role," with significantly reduced risk and cost to our military and to American taxpayers, NATO forces did not have the sophisticated means to keep up precision air attacks. Consequently, the United States continued to play a lead role in the attacks until Qaddafi was driven from power and shot some seven months later. The American humanitarian rescue mission had morphed into regime change after all.

New York Times reporter Charlie Savage recounts in his book, *Power Wars*, that when Congress returned from its recess in early April 2011 the Obama administration held a briefing for the full House and Senate in a congressional auditorium. At the briefing, Democratic representative Gerald Nadler of New York asked Secretary of State Hillary Clinton whether she agreed with him that the administration needed congressional authorization for the Libya mission. She reportedly replied, "Jerry, we don't need congressional authorization. But if Congress wants to help by passing a resolution to support it, we'd welcome it."[19]

As May 20 approached—the sixtieth day since the US mission began under the war powers time clock—White House lawyers grew increasingly nervous about the lack of congressional approval. It could not even be tied to a specific appropriations item—a hook previous administrations had used as authorization for war—because no money bills had been enacted in the interim containing line items linked to the Libyan operation.

As day fifty rolled around, the lawyers told Obama of their concerns, and Obama agreed to explore the possibility of getting congressional authorization. However, a week later, word was passed back to the White House from the Hill that there was no appetite in Congress to enact an authorization. Even though senators Kerry and McCain had previously talked about pushing a resolution, they had not yet come up with one. And seeing there was no chance of getting a resolution through the House anyway, the two senators shelved plans to push for a resolution in the Senate.

On May 17, three days before the deadline, the national security staff members for the top congressional leaders of both parties were summoned to the White House. The chiefs of staff of the top four leaders had previously been told by deputy national security adviser Denis McDonough that the continued use of armed Predator drones had triggered a threshold that created a "legal imperative" for congressional authorization. When the national security staff members arrived for the meeting with McDonough, he asked them to consider pushing through Congress a joint resolution of support for the Libya operation. When they asked him about how a "legal imperative" had been triggered, he backtracked and denied there was such a legal necessity. As Savage summarizes this bizarre switch, "the administration wanted Congress to pass an authorization without making any acknowledgement that it was, in fact, necessary." Finally, McDonough told the group that the White House had draft language they were thinking of sending to the Hill. However, it was never sent.

Instead, Obama's May 20 letter to Congress included the elliptical reference to a Kerry-McCain resolution (an unintroduced draft) as being something that would be nice to have, but not necessary. The president's thinking had again reverted to rationalizing that a congressional authorization was unnecessary because the sum total of US involvement in the mission did not rise to the level of hostilities contemplated by the sixty-day War Powers Resolution's timetable for withdrawal. This so-called nonhostilities theory was based on a four-factor test: no sustained fighting or exchanges with hostile forces; no American ground troops; no serious threat of American casualties; and no significant chance of escalation.

Savage writes that after the sixty-day deadline passed, all four congressional leaders—Boehner, Pelosi, Reid, and McConnell—"made public comments that suggested they did not think the administration was violating the War Powers Resolution."[20] Nevertheless, floor activity in the House picked up after the May 20 deadline. On May 26, the House voted 416–5 for an amendment by Democratic representative John Conyers of Michigan to the defense authorization bill, barring the use of funds for US ground troops in Libya.[21] A week later, Democratic representative Dennis Kucinich of Ohio was threatening to call up his resolution (H. Con. Res. 51), pursuant to the War Powers Resolution, to terminate US participation in the Libyan operation within fifteen days after its adoption.[22]

Speaker John Boehner, worried that the Kucinich resolution might attract considerable Republican support, hastily drafted his own alternative "sense of the House" resolution (H. Res. 292) and had the Rules Committee make it in order the next day. The special rule (H. Res. 294) provided for an hour of debate each on the Boehner and Kucinich resolutions, with the speaker's resolution to be voted on first.[23] Boehner's strategy of giving the House an opportunity to vote on a tough-sounding but toothless "sense of the House" resolution worked. In essence, it symbolically barred US ground troops and called for a report by June 16 explaining the US-Libya policy. The speaker's resolution was adopted on June 4, 268–145, with only 10 Republicans defecting. Kucinich's resolution was then rejected, 148–265, with 87 Republicans and 61 Democrats in favor. If three-fourths of House Democrats who voted had supported instead of opposed the Kucinich resolution, it would have passed, 208–205—an unlikely scenario with a Democratic president. Moreover, Boehner's argument to his own caucus, that a unilateral US withdrawal would seriously undermine the NATO alliance, was persuasive with some Democrats as well.

The May 26 House exercise on Libya did not satisfy some members as being meaningful. A little over a month later, on June 24, the House took another run at the US role in Libya, this time setting up two more substantive alternatives. Both measures were introduced just two days before floor consideration, and neither had been reported by either committee of jurisdiction—Armed Services or Foreign Affairs.

The first was a joint resolution (HJ Res. 68) introduced by Democratic Representative Alcee Hastings of Florida. It authorized the president to continue the limited use of US armed forces in Libya as part of the NATO mission but prohibited the introduction of ground troops except for rescue operations. The House rejected that resolution, 123–295, with only 8 Republicans in favor and Democrats splitting 115 for, and 70 against.

The other measure was a bill (HR 2278) introduced by Republican representative Tom Rooney of Florida that limited the use of funds to only supporting the following: search and rescue; intelligence, surveillance, and reconnaissance; aerial refueling; and operational planning. It was an attempt to confine the US role to what the president had said it would be after the initial phase of bombing—the drawdown that never happened. The Rooney measure went down to defeat as well, 180–238, with 144 Republicans in favor and 89 opposed. Democrats were overwhelmingly opposed, 36–149.[24]

The House had voted on five options since early June and could only agree on the Conyers and Boehner "no US boots on the ground" policy—something that UN Security Council Resolution 1973 already forbade. But the House could not bring itself to authorize the mission (Hastings), limit its scope (Rooney), or pull the plug (Kucinich).

Meantime, the Senate Foreign Relations Committee finally did bestir itself on June 28 to report a joint resolution by the committee's chairman, Senator John Kerry of Massachusetts, authorizing the limited use of force (the air war) against Libya in support of US national security interests, and as part of the NATO mission to enforce UN Security Council Resolution 1973. The authorization would expire when the NATO mission ended or one year after enactment, whichever came first. The measure was cosponsored by Senator John McCain and eleven other senators, only three of whom were Republicans: Lindsey Graham, Roy Blunt, and Mark Kirk.[25]

When the Senate took up a motion to consider the resolution on July 5, the only member of the Senate Foreign Relations

Committee to speak was its second-ranking Republican, Bob Corker of Tennessee. Corker succinctly laid out the case against its consideration:

> The President did not ask for what it is we are going to be debating this evening. The President earlier asked for a resolution of support [the draft sense of Senate resolution by Senators Kerry, McCain and others, that was never introduced] but not an authorization for this third war we are undertaking right now in Libya. . . . As a matter of fact, the President, in a very cutely worded letter to Congress, tried to state that we were not involved in hostilities in Libya, and he did so in order to circumvent a law that has been on the books for many years called the War Powers Act.

Although Corker said he thought the president "should be made to seek authorization," he added that there is "no way anything we do on the Senate floor—other than possibly pulling our troops out of Libya . . . is going to affect anything we are doing in Libya one iota."[26] Only four other senators participated in the debate, all Republicans who shared Corker's views.

It soon became clear that there was no interest in even debating the measure, especially in the face of a looming debt limit crisis. Consequently, Senate Majority Leader Harry Reid asked and received unanimous consent to withdraw the motion to consider the resolution and to vitiate the cloture motion (to cut off debate).[27]

The Libyan engagement is a cautionary tale of both how mission creep occurs and the unintended consequences of regime change. Driving Qaddafi from power did not culminate in the birth of a liberated and secure democratic Republic of Libya. It only produced more violence, chaos, and anarchy as competing factions fought for control of the country. The United States became a victim of this carnage when a group of Islamist terrorists attacked the

US consulate in Benghazi on September 12, 2012, killing the US ambassador to Libya, Chris Stevens, and three other Americans. This tragedy prompted a new letter to Congress from President Obama under the War Powers Resolution, this one notifying Congress that in response to the attack he had deployed to Libya "a security force from the US Africa Command . . . to support the security of US personnel in Libya."

The president used the same letter to let Congress know he had also sent "an additional security force to Yemen in response to security threats there." Both forces would remain in Libya and Yemen "until the security situation becomes such that they are no longer needed."[28] A renewed war on terrorism was heating up again across the Middle East, and Congress was again on notice.

Syria

Syria was not isolated from the Arab Spring erupting in other countries. Protests there led to civil war and retaliation by the entrenched dictatorships against the rebel forces. Although Obama had rules against arming the rebels in Syria against the Assad regime (for fear the arms would fall into the hands of Islamist extremists), he did draw a "red line" against the use by President Assad of chemical weapons against civilian populations.

It became clear in August 2013 that there had been such a chemical assault on the Damascus suburbs, killing upward of 1,500 people, including children. Although Assad denied responsibility, a preponderance of human and technical intelligence identified the Syrian government as being behind the attack. Obama declared that his red line had been crossed and called a meeting of the National Security Council to discuss a response. Most advisers said he had a responsibility to do something, although his chief of staff and longtime national security aide Denis McDonough offered a lone dissent: "I don't think this is our fight."[29]

By late August, the president was prepared to authorize a retaliatory attack. This time, however, there would be no UN Security Council Resolution to use as justification: Russia and China, who had abstained on the Libya resolutions, felt betrayed by how the authority's humanitarian purposes had been magnified to produce regime change. The president would have to act on his own, without international or even NATO sanction. Even the Parliament of America's staunchest ally, Great Britain, voted against British participation, and the prime minister said he would respect the vote.

The British demurral isolated the president even more. Although most of Obama's advisers opposed seeking authorization from Congress for the strikes on the grounds that Congress was dysfunctional and politically paralyzed, the president reconvened his National Security Council staff around 6 P.M. on Friday, August 30, and announced he was postponing the strike and would first seek congressional approval. The president publicly unveiled his decision the next day in a Rose Garden appearance, in which he confirmed he was prepared to give the order but was "also mindful that I'm the president of the world's oldest constitutional democracy." The White House sent a hastily drafted authorization resolution to the Hill that same day (Saturday, August 31). Obama also had the secretaries of state and defense brief senators by phone, and he authorized a classified briefing on Capitol Hill on Sunday.

Senior House Republican Tom Cole of Oklahoma, a close adviser to Speaker Boehner, expressed skepticism about the move, saying the president didn't have a chance to win the vote if he couldn't rally a majority of his own party in Congress; and "Democrats have been conspicuously silent. . . . He is a war president without a war party." Cole's insights proved accurate. Even Republican senators John McCain and Lindsey Graham, who had urged Obama to be more aggressive toward Syria, indicated they might not vote for his resolution because it was limited to dealing with Assad's future chemical warfare capabilities.[30]

Although the Senate Foreign Relations Committee quickly reported the requested resolution, it was not brought to the floor of the Senate because public sentiment was running heavily against intervention in Syria. This lack of public support was also reflected in strong opposition on the House side of the Capitol.

The dilemma was resolved when Russian president Vladimir Putin stepped in and brokered an agreement with Assad by which Russia would secure and remove the weapons. That proved to be acceptable to both Obama and Congress, and the immediate quandary quickly faded. However, Syria (and Iraq) would remain at center stage for the next round of American war powers debates, as a new terrorist organization began to fill the vacuum left by the US withdrawal from Iraq.[31]

ISIS

The Obama administration's views on what does and does not constitute hostilities under the War Powers Resolution was put to another test with the rise of the Islamic State of Iraq and Syria in 2014. Once again the president's ambivalence came into play. On one hand, he had argued that the 9/11 use of force resolution (aimed primarily at the Taliban and al-Qaeda in Afghanistan) was obsolete and should be repealed. On the other hand, he argued that it could suffice as authorization for action against ISIS if Congress was unable to enact a new AUMF. In a nutshell, he wanted to "halve it both ways" (pun intended).

In this instance, the executive branch's ambivalence ran up against the ambivalence of Congress as to whether a new AUMF was necessary, and, if so, what limits should be placed on it. These clashing uncertainties produced an offsetting, ambivalence equivalence, inducing a state of inaction in Congress. (Expressed as a classic paradox, it is what happens when a movable question meets an irresistible force.) Here is how it unfolded.

The United States had withdrawn most of its military forces from Iraq by 2012 pursuant to an agreement struck with the Iraqi government by Obama's predecessor, President George W. Bush. But US withdrawal was no guarantee of peace and stability. In fact, it only paved the way for increased internal strife and violence.

By 2014, there was a new bully on the block in the form of an al-Qaeda spin-off called ISIL, the Islamic State of Iraq and the Levant; or, more commonly, ISIS, the Islamic State of Iraq and Syria. The aim of this self-declared Islamic state was to establish a worldwide Islamic caliphate. Moreover, it was making rapid gains in conquering Iraqi territory that ill-prepared government troops could not defend, abandoning their weapons and fading into the woodwork.

In June 2014, ISIS militants seized control of Mosul, the third-largest city in Iraq, in an opening round blitzkrieg-like offensive that brought vast portions of that country and neighboring Syria under their control. In early August, the United States commenced air strikes against ISIS in an effort to halt its offensive. The beheadings of several Americans by ISIS turned the attention of the American people, and their elected representatives, back to the region and to the threats this relatively new terrorist organization seemed to pose.

Pressures built on President Obama to take action, but he was disinclined to reengage US forces beyond the air strikes and military aid and training the United States could provide to local forces. Despite these pressures from a group of war hawks in the Capitol, most members of Congress were not clamoring for a new war or even a vote on the issue. As the respected *CQ Almanac* put it, "The congressional debate about Iraq policy in 2014 was more about inaction than action."[32]

On September 10, 2014, the president gave a nationally televised address in which he declared, "We will degrade, and ultimately destroy, [ISIS] through a comprehensive and sustained counter-terrorism strategy." This strategy was to include a systematic campaign of air strikes against the terrorists; an increase in support to forces fighting them on the ground; the use of American counterterrorism capabilities to prevent ISIS attacks; and the continuation of humanitarian assistance to innocent civilians displaced by ISIS—all in conjunction with "a broad coalition of partners."

Although the president indicated that he already had "the authority to address the threat from [ISIS]," he believed "we are the strongest as a nation when the president and Congress work together." He therefore welcomed "congressional support for this effort in order to show the world that Americans are united in confronting this danger," without specifying the form of support he had in mind.[33]

In a follow-up letter to Congress on September 23, the president stated the air campaign against ISIS in Iraq and Syria had begun, including the deployment of 475 additional US armed forces to Iraq. He specified that the authority under which he was acting included the 2001 9/11 AUMF and the 2002 Iraq AUMF, as well as his constitutional and statutory authority as commander in chief. However, instead of requesting a formal authorization from Congress, the president's letter simply concluded, "I appreciate the support of the Congress in this action."[34] The president may have been referring to a continuing appropriations resolution Congress cleared on September 18 that included $5 billion in appropriations for military operations against the Islamic State threat, including $1.6 billion for additional training and equipment for Iraqi forces. The continuing resolution also included $500 million to train and equip Syrian rebels.

Although the administration had asked that the funds be used to enable the Syrian rebels to defend themselves against Syrian troops, Congress specified that the efforts be confined to fighting ISIS. (The program was suspended the following year when it became known only five Syrians had been trained.) By the end of

2014, some 3,000 US troops were back in Iraq, although not on the front lines.[35]

October 7, 2014, marked the sixtieth day since US war planes had begun bombing ISIS positions in Iraq, presumably setting the War Powers Resolution ticking. However, on October 15, the White House clarified that the actions did not constitute the initiation of new hostilities that would require authorization by Congress. Instead, a National Security Council spokesperson reiterated what the president had indicated in September—that the 2001 and 2002 AUMFs were sufficient authority, even though they long predated the emergence of ISIS. As one constitutional scholar observed, "the two AUMFs for 2001 and 2002 were with respect to two very different conflicts, aimed at two different enemies, pursuing very different strategies, and based on completely different legal justifications."[36]

The Obama administration had broadened the scope of the original AUMF to apply not only to those responsible for planning, authorizing, committing, aiding, or harboring those responsible for the 9/11 attacks but to global terrorism generally. The AUMF language that the Bush administration originally requested in 2001 did include such additional authority, worded as follows: "to deter and preempt any future acts of terrorism or aggression against the United States." But congressional negotiators gave an emphatic "no" to that addition, and the draft language was jettisoned.[37] The Obama administration's legal jujitsu is an example of how mission creep can beget statutory stretch, bypassing all constitutional niceties.

This changed on February 11, 2015, when the president sent to Congress a draft AUMF against ISIS. The authority would apply to "limited circumstances, such as rescue operations involving US or coalition personnel or to the use of special operations to take military actions against [ISIS] leadership." The AUMF would expire in three years and would repeal the 2002 AUMF for Iraq. Again, the president asserted in his letter that he already had sufficient authority to carry out these limited military activities, but added: "I have repeatedly expressed my commitment to working with the Congress to pass a bipartisan authorization for the use of military force (AUMF) against [ISIS]." At the same time, the president called on Congress "to refine, and ultimately repeal the 2001 AUMF.

So what changed? For one thing, Congress was previously reluctant to act on a use of force resolution without specific statutory language from the president. It was not enough for the president to hint from time to time that it would be nice to have congressional support for the mission. Second, the prospect that limited ground combat operations might be necessary in Syria would potentially expand the scope of US involvement. As the president explained, the authorization "would provide the flexibility to conduct ground combat operations in other, more limited circumstances," such as rescue missions and military actions against ISIS leaders.[38]

In a White House press conference that same day, the president did make clear the AUMF did not call for the deployment of ground troops in Iraq and Syria: "I am convinced that the US should not get back into another ground war in the Middle East—it's not in our national security interests and not necessary for us to defeat [ISIS]," he told reporters. The resolution specifically forbade "enduring offensive ground combat operations."[39]

Although there was reportedly broad general support for a formal AUMF in Congress, the devil was in the details, and that is why any prospect for consensus evaporated. Republicans criticized the draft resolution as too limited, and Democrats were leery of even limited ground combat operational authority and the three-year duration of the authorization.

House Speaker Boehner said in a statement that any AUMF "must give our military commanders the flexibility and authorities they need to succeed and protect our people," and he was concerned that "the president's request does not meet this standard."

Democratic leader Nancy Pelosi, conversely, stressed the need for "something that would limit the power of the president . . . while protecting the American people in a very strong way."[40]

The House Armed Services Committee held a hearing on the president's AUMF on February 26, 2015, and the Senate Foreign Relations Committee did so on March 11, 2015. By one count, there were seventeen hearings in Congress in 2014 and 2015 on the need for an AUMF against ISIS, but no further action was taken by any of the four principal committees.[41] Members of both bodies were in no rush to introduce, cosponsor, or act on an AUMF.

In both the 113th and 114th Congresses, six AUMF measures were introduced, with a total of fifteen and twenty-two cosponsors, respectively. The leading proponents of congressional action on an AUMF in both Congresses were senators Tim Kaine of Virginia and Jeff Flake of Arizona. Their 2015 AUMF closely tracked that recommended by the president, including a three-year sunset and the limited use of ground combat troops to protect the lives of US citizens (unlike Obama's resolution, it provided no exception for action against ISIS leaders).[42]

By the spring of 2015, reporters were already writing obituaries for Obama's proposed AUMF, based on House Majority Leader Kevin McCarthy's assessment: "I do not see a path to 218 with what the president sent up because the world has become more dangerous since he laid out Yemen as the strategy of how to move forward." The reporter attributed McCarthy's doubts to the lack of pressure from voters on Congress to act on a war powers resolution. Still, McCarthy did not dismiss the possibility that the committees of jurisdiction might work out a bipartisan AUMF alternative in the weeks ahead.[43]

An opinion piece in *The Atlantic* drew the same conclusions from McCarthy's remarks about prospects for the president's measure, but it also quoted aides to Speaker Boehner as saying GOP leaders were still interested in passing "a real, robust AUMF that reflects a real, over-arching strategy to accomplish what the president says is the goal of destroying ISIS."[44]

Interest was reignited in the fall of 2015 with President Obama's decision to send fifty US special operations troops into Syria in an advisory capacity. Democrats pounced on the announcement that seemed to go beyond Obama's earlier pledge in his draft AUMF to limit boots on the ground in Syria to rescue and actions against ISIS leaders. Senator Kaine put it bluntly: "It is time for Congress to do its most solemn job, to debate and declare war."[45]

On December 6, 2015, four days after the terrorist attack in San Bernardino, California, killing fourteen people—and less than a month after 130 people were killed in coordinated terrorist attacks in Paris—President Obama gave a nationally televised address from the Oval Office on Keeping the American People Safe. In his remarks, he discussed the steps being taken to combat terrorism. Not surprisingly, he again called on Congress to pass an authorization for the use of force against ISIS: "I think it's time for Congress to vote to demonstrate the American people are united, and committed to this fight."[46]

Senate Majority Leader Mitch McConnell introduced an AUMF resolution in January 2016, with four cosponsors: senators Graham, Coats, Hatch, and Ernst. It was open ended in terms of authority and duration. McConnell used his prerogative as leader to have it placed directly on the calendar, but no further action was taken on it in the 114th Congress.[47] Other than Senator McConnell's AUMF alternative, interest in taking action on any version again waned as presidential politics took center stage.

Nevertheless, stalwart Senator Kaine prepared to make a last-ditch stand on the issue in the 114th Congress by filing two amendments in June to the pending fiscal 2017 National Defense Authorization Act. The first amendment, cosponsored by Senator Flake, would incorporate into the bill the AUMF language from their previously introduced bill. The second amendment, cosponsored by Senator Jeff Merkley (D-OR), required the next president to propose a rewritten and updated AUMF within two years, and repeal the 2001 AUMF.[48] Neither amendment was offered on the floor. Kaine would be away from the Senate for the remainder of the 114th Congress after being tapped in July by Democratic presidential nominee Hillary Clinton to be her vice presidential running mate.

In December 2016, President Obama filed his final six-month "Supplemental War Powers Letter" to Congress, summing up the "deployments of US armed forces equipped for combat." All told, the United States was militarily positioned in fourteen-plus countries around the world. In Afghanistan there were still 9,800 troops; in Iraq, more than 5,000; and in Syria, 300 special forces troops served in a training and advisory capacity. Other countries where the United States had a military presence included Turkey, Somalia, Yemen, Libya, Cuba, Jordan, Niger, Cameroon, Egypt, and Kosovo.[49]

Obama's parting gift to Congress (and to his successor, Donald J. Trump) on December 5, 2016, was a sixty-one-page "Report on the Legal and Policy Frameworks Guiding the United States' Use of Military Force and Related National Security Operations."[50] It is an amalgam of the often competing and varying rationales and justifications used by the administration for military interventions undertaken around the world over the previous eight years. Or, as an accompanying "fact sheet" put it: "The report provides in one place an articulation of the legal and policy frameworks which previously have been found across numerous speeches, public statements, reports and other materials"—the result of "eight years of sustained work by this administration to ensure that all US national security operations are conducted within a legal and policy framework that is lawful, effective and consistent with our national interests and values."[51] It was a final attempt to draw into a coherent whole the evolving Obama doctrine—an eight-year work in progress—so that future presidents and Congresses might have a clearer map for acting in differing international conflicts. The report included a country-by-country breakdown of the Obama doctrine's "application to key theaters"—Afghanistan, Iraq, Syria, Somalia, Libya, and Yemen—and the durable utility of the 2001 AUMF to justify American involvement.

Not surprisingly, reaction on the Hill was mixed. House Democratic whip Steny Hoyer praised the president for increasing "transparency and accountability" by "setting in one document a lasting legacy of his commitment to ensuring that those who serve us in national security faithfully adhere to the values and principles for which many of our young men and women in uniform gave their lives throughout our history."[52] Ranking House Intelligence Committee Democrat Adam Schiff of California qualified his praise: "I do not agree with all of the legal and policy positions outlined in this important memorandum; . . . but the document provides a high standard of transparency and adherence to the law that should be emulated by other administrations and nations."[53]

The headlines in two Washington newspapers perhaps best captured the overall thrust of the report and its portents for the future. From the *Washington Post*: "Obama Legacy: Handing Trump Broad View of War Powers"; and from the *Washington Times*: "Obama Evades Congress, Stretches War Powers in Precedent for Trump."[54] At least in the first three months of the Trump administration, no request for a new AUMF has been forthcoming from the White House; nor have the leaders of either party in Congress stepped forward to offer one. The Obama legacy endures.

6

Congress and the Iran Nuclear Deal

Rational Reactor or Design Flaw?

DURING THE LAST TWO centuries, presidents have jealously guarded their prerogatives over the conduct of American foreign policy. At the same time, Congress has exercised a check on the president's foreign policies through control of the purse strings, oversight, and legislative conditions and constraints. Moreover, the Senate has prided itself on its exclusive role in confirming US ambassadors to other countries and ratifying treaties with other nations. To circumvent Senate interference in matters of trade, in recent years, presidents have relied more on executive agreements—which do not require Senate ratification—than on treaties, squeezing the Senate out of its traditional advise and consent role.

One such agreement was struck in 2015 between the United States, five other nations, and Iran to curb Iran's ability to militarize its nuclear resources. This agreement faced scrutiny and skepticism from members of Congress who were wary of Iran's reliability and the agreement's enforceability. A handful of Republicans introduced legislation in 2014 to give Congress a vote on the proposed agreement, a concept strongly opposed by President

Obama. To the president's surprise, a modified version of the congressional review legislation gained bipartisan support in the Senate in 2015, and Obama was ultimately forced to sign into law the "Iran Nuclear Agreement Review Act."

Unlike Congress's reluctance to exercise its war powers, Congress's security concerns about nuclear proliferation fueled congressional interest and involvement in the Iran nuclear issue. The bipartisan agreement enacted is an example of how, even in the campaign culture of modern Congresses, agreement across the aisle can be reached as long as both sides can claim victory. In this instance, the Democrats ultimately protected the president's position under the review process, and the Republicans secured meaningful oversight and a formal action role on something that Congress would otherwise have been shut out of completely.

On July 14, 2015, Iran reached an agreement with the United States and five other nations to limit its nuclear program in exchange for relief from trade and nuclear sanctions. The negotiating group is referred to in shorthand as the P5+1 because it consists of the five permanent members of the UN Security Council—the United States, China, Russia, France, and the United Kingdom—plus Germany. The agreement brought to a temporary end, it was hoped, nearly two decades of Iran's attempt to develop nuclear weapons (although Iran had steadfastly maintained that its nuclear program had always been for peaceful purposes).

The US Congress has followed developments in Iran closely ever since the overthrow of the shah of Iran in 1979 and his replacement by the Ayatollah Khomeini's Islamic Republic of Iran. Attention under Khomeini initially focused on the fate of the fifty-two American diplomats and other citizens held hostage in the US Embassy in Tehran by a group the radical students for 444 days. (They were finally released minutes after Ronald Reagan was sworn in as president in 1981.)

Since then, Congresses and administrations have focused on the potential threat of Iran developing nuclear weapons.

Robert Litwak, a former National Security Council nonproliferation expert, describes the concern as follows: "The dilemma of the Iranian nuclear challenge is that Iran has mastered uranium enrichment: centrifuges that spin to produce low-enriched uranium . . . for nuclear power reactors can keep spinning to yield highly enriched uranium . . . for bombs."[1]

That is especially troublesome because Iran is considered an "outlier state" or "rogue nation," given its active assistance to terrorist organizations. In 1984, the US State Department added Iran to the department's watch list of state sponsors of terrorism, resulting in the automatic imposition of tough sanctions. The combustible combination of nuclear weapons and terrorism poses a stark danger to peace and security in the volatile Middle East and to the rest of the world. As Litwak explains, the purpose of P5+1 nuclear diplomacy was to contain Iran's nuclear program, not eliminate it, so that Iran would retain an option, or hedge, for a nuclear weapon and other nations would have a sufficient breakout period (say, twelve months) to mobilize an international response.[2]

In 1992, Congress enacted the Iran-Iraq Arms Nonproliferation Act, prohibiting the transfer of controlled goods or technology that might contribute to Iran's proliferation of advanced conventional weapons. In 1996 Congress enacted the Iran-Libya Sanctions Act, penalizing foreign and US investment exceeding $20 million annually in Iran's energy sectors. However, as with other important issues that wax and wane in the nation's capital, Congress's attention to the Iran nuclear program flagged somewhat after Iran signed onto the international nuclear safeguards protocol in 2003, agreeing to suspend its uranium enrichment and reprocessing activities and allowing monitoring of its nuclear program by the International Atomic Energy Agency.

As early as 2004, Iran was discovered cheating on its pledges, and in 2006 the International Atomic Energy Agency referred Iran's noncompliance with the safeguards to the UN Security Council.

In June 2006, the P5+1 proposed to Iran a framework for agreement that included incentives to halt its enrichment work. The following month the Security Council adopted a resolution making the calls for suspending enrichment binding for the first time.

When President Barack Obama took office in 2009, one his first priorities was a thorough review of US–Iran policy. This review led to the US joining in the P5+1 talks with Iran—a reversal from the Bush administration's policy of not participating until Iran first met the UN Security Council demands. When a US-initiated "fuel swap" proposal was offered later that year, it fell through due to opposition from an opposing political faction in Iran. This failure led the UN Security Council to vote on June 9, 2010, to expand sanctions against Iran, banning it from conducting nuclear-capable ballistic missile tests and imposing an arms embargo on the transfer of major weapons systems to Iran.[3]

This chapter traces Congress's growing role in the ongoing maneuvering to prevent Iran from developing nuclear weapons, notwithstanding the Obama administration's insistence that Congress stay out of the way during the delicate P5+1 talks. The president explained that he was pursuing an executive agreement, which did not require congressional approval.[4]

That only raised hackles on Capitol Hill, resulting in an entirely new level of congressional involvement—one neither requested nor contemplated by the administration. In this chapter, I will not thrash through the technical and diplomatic weeds of negotiations but instead concentrate on the constitutional struggle between the branches for the privilege of shaping America's foreign policy toward Iran.[5]

Congress Steps In

On June 24, 2010, Congress followed the UN Security Council's lead from earlier that month by enacting the Comprehensive Iran

Sanctions, Accountability, and Divestment Act. This act tightened sanctions on firms investing in Iran's energy sector and extended them until 2016. President Barack Obama's State Department, initially wary of the measure when it was first introduced earlier in the year, called on Senate Foreign Relations Committee chairman John Kerry (D-MA) to delay action. Nevertheless, the bill sailed through the House and Senate by lopsided majorities in March and April 2010, respectively. The conference report on the bill passed the Senate on June 24 by a vote of 99–0, and later that same day passed the House, 408–8. The president signed it into law on July 1, 2010.[6]

In January 2014, the P5+1 and Iran approved a Joint Plan of Action, paving the way for work on a comprehensive agreement. Sensing the imminence of a final deal, members of Congress began laying the groundwork for their own action plan. Leading the way in the Senate was Republican senator Bob Corker of Tennessee, the ranking minority member on the Foreign Relations Committee. Corker introduced the Iran Nuclear Negotiations Act in July 2014, with eleven cosponsors, all Republicans. The Democrats on the committee, who were still in the majority for another five months, held back in deference to President Obama and the committee's former chairman, John Kerry, now secretary of state.

In his floor remarks on introducing the bill, Corker said he supported the negotiations and the president's goal of preventing Iran from obtaining a nuclear weapon, but his purpose in introducing the legislation was to send a simple message: "Allow Congress to weigh in on behalf of the American people on what is one of the most important national security issues facing our Nation."[7] No hearings were held or further action taken on the measure in the 113th Congress, but an opening shot had been fired over the bow of a resistant White House.

Crunch Time in the 114th Congress

On February 27, 2015, shortly after the 114th Congress convened, Senator Corker reintroduced a modified version of his 2014 bill. The new bill was titled the "Iran Nuclear Agreement Review Act of 2015."[8] Since Corker's first effort the previous year, Republicans had retaken control of the Senate, elevating Corker to the chairmanship of the Foreign Relations Committee. The former chairman, Senator Robert Menendez of New Jersey, was forced to step down from the top Democratic position in April 2015 due to an indictment for corruption. He was replaced by Senator Ben Cardin of Maryland as the ranking minority member. This time, Corker had a bipartisan list of cosponsors when he introduced his bill—five Republicans and six Democrats, including committee Democrats Menendez and Senator Tim Kaine of Virginia. Cardin did not join as an original cosponsor, likely because he was new to being the top Democrat on the committee and had some responsibility to work with the president.

One thing that had not changed was President Obama's opposition to any interference from Congress. The day after Corker introduced his bill, presidential spokeswoman Bernadette Meehan of the National Security Council staff announced that the president did not think the time was right for Congress to pass additional legislation on Iran. "If this bill is sent to the President," she said, "he will veto it." She explained: "We should give our negotiators the best chance of success, rather than complicating their efforts." Corker promptly issued a statement that the president's veto threat was "disappointing."[9]

Two things happened in Congress in early March 2015 that complicated things on Capitol Hill, and, indirectly, with the administration and the P5+1 negotiations with Iran. On March 3, Israeli prime minister Benjamin Netanyahu addressed a joint meeting of Congress at the invitation of Speaker Boehner—over

the clear opposition of the administration. The timing of Netanyahu's appearance as the nuclear agreement negotiations neared
completion brought home to many members the concern that
many of their Jewish American constituents expressed about the
threat Iran posed to Israel's existence. Indeed, the Israeli prime
minister devoted his entire speech to the subject of Iran and the
pending nuclear agreement, which he said "leaves Iran with a vast
nuclear infrastructure," and "a real danger that Iran could get to
the bomb by violating the deal." Moreover, he added, "an even
greater danger" will be posed in about a decade when the deal
expires: "Iran would then be free to build a huge nuclear capacity
that could produce many, many nuclear bombs."[10]

The second bombshell to drop occurred on March 9 with
release of an "open letter" to the leaders of Iran from Republican
Senator Tom Cotton of Arkansas and forty-six of his Senate GOP
colleagues. (The only Republicans who did not sign were senators
Lamar Alexander and Bob Corker, both of Tennessee.) There was
an immediate outcry—from the White House, in the media, and
among congressional Democrats—charging Cotton and company
with interfering with ongoing negotiations.[11]

An actual reading of the letter, however, as I noted in a column at
the time, "reveals little more than what could have been an executive summary of a Congressional Research Service report on the differences between treaties, congressional-executive agreements and
executive agreements, and their relative legal significance." Cotton's main point was that the agreement being negotiated was "a
mere executive agreement," not subject to approval by Congress—
something that "the next president could revoke . . . with the stroke
of a pen." Moreover, the terms of the agreement, wrote Cotton,
could be modified by future Congresses at any time.[12]

On April 2, Iran and the P5+1 announced agreement on a gen-
eral framework that outlined the parameters of a nuclear deal.[13]
Two weeks later, on April 14, the day on which the Senate Foreign
Relations Committee was scheduled to markup the Corker bill,

two significant events occurred. First, Cardin joined with Corker in introducing a compromise amendment in the nature of a substitute that would be used as the base text for amendment purposes. Second, even though Secretary of State Kerry had been on the Hill that morning urging committee Democrats to oppose the bill, the president changed his position from opposition to support. White House spokesman Josh Earnest explained the switch: "We've gone from a piece of legislation that the president would veto to a piece of legislation that's undergone substantial revision such that it's now in the form of a compromise that the president would be willing to sign." Despite this assertion, the compromise's chief cosponsor, Senator Cardin, told reporters that "the fundamental provisions of the legislation had not changed."[14]

What had changed was growing bipartisan support for the bill. Corker had picked up fifty-five more cosponsors, for a total of sixty-six cosponsors—forty-five Republicans and twenty-one Democrats—which gave him a veto-proof majority of sixty-seven senators (counting Corker).[15] This, more than any minor tweaks in the Corker-Cardin compromise, was responsible for the president's flipping. The committee proceeded to markup and report the bill on April 14 by a unanimous vote of 19–0.[16] No committee report was issued on the measure.

The major changes that explained Democrats' willingness to sign on had actually been made between Corker's 2014 bill and the bill he introduced on February 27, 2015. The most significant revision involved dropping the expedited procedures for House and Senate consideration of a resolution disapproving an agreement, and instead attaching them to a later section of the bill relating to congressional action on reinstating sanctions if Iran violated the agreement (the so-called snapback process).

The expedited procedures Corker drew on in both bills, sometimes called "fast-track consideration," are boilerplate House and Senate procedural language found in numerous statutes designed to allow certain executive branch decisions or recommendations to be subject to up-or-down votes in the House and Senate on joint resolutions of approval or disapproval.[17] They usually involve an automatic discharge of a joint resolution of approval or disapproval from committee if not reported within a specified time; an automatic vote on a motion to proceed to consideration without debate; a specified time limit on debate in both houses; and a prohibition on amendments, dilatory motions, or motions to recommit the joint resolution to committee. Such procedures guarantee a final vote by both houses without intervening opportunities to obstruct, delay, or divert.

By dropping the expedited procedures for considering the Iran nuclear agreement in the Senate, Corker's new bill opened the door to all manner of dilatory tactics, including the possibility of a filibuster, which can only be overcome by adopting a cloture motion requiring a sixty-vote majority of senators to cut off debate.

The mystery of how these changes appeared in the new bill was solved during the first day of floor debate on the bill. As Senator Kaine explained it, in January 2015, he, Corker, and five other senators took a trip to the Middle East, where they visited officials in Saudi Arabia, Qatar, and Israel. At some point during the trip, Corker asked Kaine why he had not cosponsored Corker's 2014 bill if, as he claimed, he thought Congress should play a role on the Iran agreement process. Kaine said he replied: " 'You are absolutely right [on] congressional approval; but there are some aspects of the bill I don't like.' The chairman said to me: 'Then, fine, you rewrite it or propose amendments, and let's see if we can work together.' "

Kaine continued: "So I did and others did, and we put our best good faith down on the table. We found a listening ear. . . . Senators on both sides of the aisle willing to try to exercise that congressional approval role . . . in the right way, not the wrong way." And that rewrite of the 2014 bill, Kaine concluded, is what was contained in the bill Corker introduced on February 27, 2015.[18]

In the same debate, Cardin confirmed Kaine's account, thanking him and Corker "for giving us a good model as to how legislation should be developed." Cardin went on to indicate his role: "I was proud to work with Senator Corker so that we could get the White House and get some of our members who didn't share enthusiasm of this legislation, to a place where they are comfortable in supporting the bill."[19]

The president knew when he was outnumbered and it was time to fold. The Corker-Cardin "compromise" was a convenient crutch to lean on as he shifted positions. As Senate Majority Leader Mitch McConnell put it that same day, "Who would have imagined that the White House, after trying to kill this bipartisan bill for months, would find itself forced to pull a near-total about-face."[20]

The Senate Uses a Bait-and-Switch Tactic

The Senate was the lead actor on the Iran nuclear agreement review bill. The House had not bothered introducing a companion bill and awaited the Senate's move. Ironically, the Senate incorporated the language of the Foreign Relations Committee's nuclear review bill into an unrelated House bill: the "Protecting Volunteer Firefighters and Emergency Responders Act"—"a bill (HR 1191) to amend the Internal Revenue Code of 1986 to ensure that emergency services volunteers are not taken into account as employees under the shared responsibility requirements contained in the Patient Protection and Affordable Care Act."

Although the original House bill, as introduced by Representative Lou Barletta (R-PA) had only twenty-three cosponsors and had not been reported from committee, it was sufficiently noncontroversial to be considered under a suspension of the rules (forty minutes of debate, no amendments, and a two-thirds vote required for passage). It was called up by Ways and Means Committee chairman Paul Ryan on March 16 and overwhelmingly passed the House, 415–0.[21]

In the Senate, the firefighters' bill was held at the desk and placed on the legislative calendar on March 19 (instead of being referred to committee). It was called up on the floor on April 23, and Senator Corker immediately offered an amendment in the nature of a substitute consisting of the text of the Iran Nuclear Agreement Review Act reported by his committee on April 14.[22]

Why does the Senate sometimes insert legislative language from one of its bills into an unrelated House-passed bill? Although it may look like a bait-and-switch tactic, there is no intended subterfuge— no one would be fooled for long. Nor is it the same thing as substituting Senate language into a House "companion" bill to facilitate going to conference with the other body. In a column at the time, I characterized the Iran review language's relationship with the firefighters' tax bill this way: "Instead of a companion [bill] we are talking about third cousins, twice removed—very distant relatives at best."[23]

The seemingly irrational act has a rational explanation, and it is found in the Constitution's "origination clause," which requires revenue-related measures to originate in the House. Because the House had not acted on a comparable Iran bill, and because the Senate measure contained revenue components (relating to sanctions), the Senate hitched a ride on the House-passed volunteer firefighters tax measure as the next best thing.

Had the Senate sent the Coker bill to the House, it would have risked having the bill sent back with a "blue-slip" resolution attached. Blue-slip resolutions (because they are printed on blue paper) assert that the Senate has violated one of the constitutional prerogatives of the House and the measure is therefore being returned without further action. In my column I conclude: "Although some may wonder about such unusual procedural contortions to satisfy origination clause concerns, that is exactly what happened and why. For those attempting to follow the process, it is a taxing experience."[24]

Approving the Disapproval Process

When Corker called up his substitute amendment on April 23, 2015, he knew his biggest challenge would be to ward off threatening amendments (sometimes called "poison pill" amendments because they could jeopardize the bill's chances of passage and approval by the president). Menendez, in his opening floor remarks, perhaps best expressed the need to hold the delicate, bipartisan package together: "I respect everybody's views and everybody's rights to have amendments. . . . But I will oppose amendments . . . that I consider to be poisonous and that undermine the very essence of what we have accomplished in the Foreign Relations Committee."[25]

Notwithstanding the dangers certain amendments posed to the bipartisan compromise, Corker also supported senators' rights to offer amendments under an open process. However, opposition to the nuclear agreement was running high among some Republicans. Of the eighty-six amendments filed on the bill, seventy-six were sponsored by Republicans.[26] Over the course of the first eight days of debate in late April and early May, only nine amendments had been offered. On May 5 Majority Leader McConnell filed a cloture motion to bring consideration to a close. Two days later, the Senate voted 93–6 to invoke cloture (end debate).

Before that only two amendments had been voted on. The first amendment, by Wisconsin Republican senator Ron Johnson, would deem any agreement reached to be a treaty subject to a two-thirds Senate vote for ratification. It was rejected, 39–57 (with no Democrats in support and 12 Republicans in opposition). The second amendment, offered by Republican senator John Barrasso of Wyoming, would require the president to include in his certification report every ninety days whether Iran was directly responsible for any terrorist acts against the United States or any of its citizens. It was rejected, 45–54, with no Democrats voting for the amendment and only 8 Republicans voting against.[27]

After cloture was invoked, four of the seven remaining pending amendments fell on germaneness points of order; one amendment was withdrawn; and one, by Corker, changing the bill's title, was adopted by unanimous consent. Finally, the Corker-Cardin substitute, as amended, was adopted, 98–1. Arkansas Republican Tom Cotton was the lone dissenting senator.[28]

In the House, Foreign Affairs Committee chairman Ed Royce called up the Senate-passed bill under suspension of the rules on May 14 (after getting unanimous consent to extend debate time from forty minutes to one hour). The measure easily surpassed the two-thirds vote threshold for passage, 400–25. The president signed the bill into law on May 22, without issuing a signing statement.[29]

Agreeing to Disagree

Although Congress is still capable of forging bipartisan compromises on process matters, the body today is probably more divided than ever regarding where any statutory process should lead substantively. Congressional action on the actual Iran Nuclear Agreement is a case in point.

On July 14, 2015, Iran and the P5+1 announced a comprehensive deal, the Joint Comprehensive Plan of Action. Five days later, as required by the review law, Obama sent the package to Congress. That started the sixty-day review clock ticking, with an expiration date of September 17 (Constitution Day in the United States). The UN Security Council endorsed the nuclear pact and the lifting of Security Council sanctions on Iran pending the completion of certain steps.

Under the law, the first thirty days of the congressional review period are reserved for committee hearings and briefings. So it was not until September 8 that the agreement finally was called up for Senate floor action. Earlier that day, however, Minority Leader

Harry Reid used his morning hour time to lay out his position in favor of the Iran Nuclear Agreement. He inserted in the *Congressional Record* a speech on the agreement that he delivered at the Carnegie Endowment for International Peace that same morning.

In his speech, Reid indicated that it was clear to him and to "the overwhelming majority of my caucus that this agreement gives us the best chance to avoid one of the worst threats in today's world—a nuclear-armed Iran." While praising the Iran review act, Reid made clear the process does not oblige senators to vote for a specific outcome because, under the terms of the review act, the Senate has the option of approving, disapproving, or taking no action. Reid then informed colleagues that "Democrats have already agreed to forgo our opportunity to filibuster," provided Majority Leader McConnell allows for "the chance to go straight to a vote on passage of the resolution" and agrees to a sixty-vote majority for adoption of the disapproval resolution.

Reid went on to quote Senator Kaine, one of the authors of the review act, who had indicated in remarks delivered earlier that day that the bill "was drafted so that 60 votes would be required in the Senate to pass either a motion of approval or a motion of disapproval." Reid backed up that claim by quoting Senator Cotton, the lone dissenting vote on the review act, who, in Reid's words, said that "the reason he didn't vote for it was because it required a 60-vote threshold."[30] Although the review act did not directly require a sixty-vote majority to pass a disapproval resolution, the Senate practice is to require such a vote in return for not having to go through the sixty-vote cloture process to end a filibuster.

Majority Leader McConnell again employed the bait-and-switch tactic to avoid a blue-slip rejection by the House of the disapproval measure (again, because it was considered a revenue measure). This time, the vehicle he used was a House-passed joint resolution—the "Hire More Heroes Act"—a tax measure exempting certain TRICARE and Department of Veterans Affairs employees from being counted for purposes of the employer mandate of the Affordable Care Act. McConnell immediately offered the agreement disapproval language as an amendment in the nature of a substitute, and then proceeded to fill the amendment tree with seven minor amendments to block others from offering amendments.[31]

Senate debate continued over eight legislative days with McConnell offering and withdrawing multiple amendments, motions to recommit with instructions, and cloture motions. Of the four cloture votes taken on September 10 and 15, the first one was the high-water mark, with 58 votes for cloture—two short of the 60-vote threshold to end debate. (The three subsequent cloture votes only mustered 56, 53, and 56 votes, respectively.) The final two cloture votes occurred on September 17, the final day of the 60-day review period. The bill had died a death by deadline.

The initial plan in the House was to also consider a disapproval resolution. House Foreign Affairs Committee chairman Ed Royce (R-CA) introduced such a resolution on August 4, with no prior committee consideration. On August 8, the Rules Committee reported a special rule for the disapproval resolution that allowed for ten hours of general debate and no amendments.[32] However, neither the rule nor joint resolution were ever called up in the House. The reason, as I noted in a column at the time, was that "some eager legal beavers in the GOP caucus glommed onto a provision in the review bill requiring congressional access to all relevant documents, including any classified annexes. They claimed that the president had not turned over a secret inspection document, and therefore that the congressional review period had not legally begun."[33]

This controversy forced Republican leaders to withdraw the Royce disapproval resolution and scramble to devise fallback measures relating to the Iran deal. What emerged, literally overnight, were three hastily drafted options under the umbrella of a special rule (H. Res. 412) from the Rules Committee, reported on September 10. The rule made in order the consideration of three overnight deliveries, barring amendments to all three.

The first measure (H. Res. 411) was a "sense of the House" resolution introduced by Kansas Republican representative Mike Pompeo—one of the "eager legal beavers" alluded to previously—finding the president not in compliance with the Iran Nuclear Agreement Review Act because he had not sent to Congress all the documents relating to the agreement. After two hours of debate, the resolution was adopted, 245–183, with every Republican voting "aye" and every Democrat voting "nay."

The second measure (HR 3461), introduced by House Speaker John Boehner (R-OH), would approve the Joint Comprehensive Plan of Action relating to the nuclear program of Iran—one of the options available under the review act (even though it contradicted the finding of the previously adopted resolution that the review clock had not yet started ticking). Although Boehner opposed his own resolution, he thought members should at least be able to cast a direct vote for or against the agreement, especially after arguing so strenuously for some kind of congressional participation in the agreement process. After three hours of debate, Boehner's approval resolution was rejected by the House, 162–269, with no Republicans voting for it, and only 25 Democrats voting against it.

The third measure (HR 3460), introduced by Congressman Peter Roskam (R-IL), would prohibit the president from waiving, suspending, reducing, or providing any relief from the application of sanctions pursuant to the Iran nuclear agreement, before January 21, 2017. The measure was obviously timed to allow the next president, on or after his inauguration day in 2017, to make the decision. After two hours of debate, the bill passed the House, 247–186, on September 11, with only two Democrats in favor, and no Republicans opposing.[34]

What Did It Matter?

Any outside observer who bothered, for whatever reason, to watch this bizarre, contorted process unfold—from passage of the review act to debate on the agreement itself—would probably shrug and conclude that it was an exercise in folly, signifying little. The president was practically guaranteed to get his agreement, regardless of Congress. His undisguised resentment of Congress's noisy and nosy interference with his diplomatic negotiating prerogatives was palpable—right up to the time he saw the writing on the wall (in longhand arithmetic) and embraced the process, albeit, at arm's length.

The president neither won outright approval of the agreement, nor did he suffer a bicameral disapproval that would have triggered a nasty veto override fight. Although his veto likely would have been sustained, his stature as president would have been diminished in the eyes of the world.

The review process legislation was approved overwhelmingly by virtue of a truly bipartisan effort to forge a compromise acceptable to both parties and, ultimately, to the president. The various House and Senate votes on the plan itself, conversely, were nearly all along straight party lines. The important issue for both sides was that Congress did assert itself to play a role in the agreement process, notwithstanding the president's initial objections. Moreover, the resulting process compromise required quarterly reports by the president on Iran's compliance, ensuring that Congress could closely monitor developments over the ten-year duration of the agreement, and, if there is a breach in compliance, to move quickly to reinstate sanctions. (The expedited snapback provisions for restoring sanctions is a major substantive win for Congress.)

Notwithstanding the frustrations and disappointments many members experienced with the ultimate outcomes, the answer to the question posed by this chapter's subhead is that Congress was a rational reactor to the challenge to play some role and not the unwitting dupe of a design flaw. Without Senator Kaine's compromise efforts, there would have been no review act. Without Senate Cardin's lobbying, there would have been no bipartisan majority (or presidential signature). And without Senator Corker's openness to bipartisan compromise, there would have been neither. This is in contrast to Congress's reluctance, as demonstrated in the previous chapter, to recapture its war power under the Constitution. The stakes are higher and much more immediate on questions of war. That is why Congress prefers blame avoidance on questions of war as opposed to sharing responsibility and accountability with the commander in chief.

The Iran process compromise also may be an indication that Congress is beginning to awaken to its institutional and constitutional responsibilities, and the experience may serve as a confidence-building block for future challenges. As Senator Cardin pointed out, senators Corker and Kaine have provided Congress with a model of how successful legislation can be developed. Only time will tell.

7

Governing in a Political World

THIS BOOK BEGAN ALMOST as an indictment of partisan majorities in Congress for manipulating the rules to produce preferred political outcomes. The more I explored various case studies on major legislation, the more apparent it became that procedures had evolved to adapt to partisan realities and needs rather than that partisanship had changed outcomes due to procedural manipulation. The old saw on Capitol Hill—at least in the House of Representatives—is that a determined majority can always work its will. Procedures simply help accelerate this process.

To some, this may seem to be a chicken-and-egg question—which came first, the partisanship or the procedural fixes. To others, it does not matter because both causes and effects reinforce each other to such an extent that the causal source is irrelevant. They are inseparable and indistinguishable forces. The central question is: At what point do procedural fixes become procedural abuses of the minority party and individual members by denying them full participation in the legislative process?

This is a matter of some controversy and depends on where you stand—in the majority, or in the minority. Both parties engage in the same behavior when they move from minority to majority, and it has become the acceptable way of doing things, even though the minority protests by voting against such procedural special rules—or, in the Senate, against invoking cloture. With both parties knowing that their roles could be reversed after the next election, they have no illusions that the same constraining treatment will not be visited on the new minority. Therefore, neither party has an incentive to be fairer. Instead, the noose is simply tightened.

In some distant past, if not a golden era, the two parties fought over their differences on a particular bill and eventually found a way to resolve those differences, both within and between the two chambers. The goal was to find common ground on which to produce a law, and the procedures for getting there were more open and fairer, and less partisan, than in recent times. Today, given the widening rift between the parties, there is little hope for either house or either party to come together on anything, but especially on major policy problems, and certainly not on the procedural treatment of their opponents.

What are the alternatives? Either the two parties' differences could magically fade into a blue mist hanging between them, which is not likely, or one party could become so dominant that the minority party would be marginalized and need to content itself with occasional legislative crumbs from the majority's table. Again, this scenario is unlikely in the foreseeable future given the near 50/50 partisan split in the electorate. A third possibility is that a new, bipartisan consensus could emerge at the outbreak of a major crisis, forcing the two parties to devise new ways to come together to deal swiftly and effectively with the crisis.

This might entail embracing new ways of looking at the legislative process that involve listening to the views of others, treating them with respect, and even accepting some of the opponents' proposals as part of a grand bargain to solve the problem. Such a process would surely be noticed by the public as being a departure from politics as usual—the fierce and noisy infighting that often leads nowhere—and might even be rewarded by the people and embraced as part of a new, national policy consensus.

If all this sounds too good to happen, it probably is—at least for very long. Crisis responses occur out of necessity and are unsustainable over time because the sense of urgency and pressures for action recede. As a crisis is dealt with and normalcy returns, bipartisan goodwill vanishes and old partisan ways return. Neither party wants to give the other party credit for solving anything. Parties are about winning elections and occupying seats of power. Each party hopes to convince the electorate at the next election that there will be a difference between it and the other party—that party X has better ideas than party Y and therefore can address problems more successfully and effectively. Sharing credit only confuses, contradicts, and dilutes the power of this narrative.

One is left with what we might call a Hatfield and McCoy standoff—two feuding clans on opposing mountaintops, only capable of shouting insults at each other across the wide divide and unable and unwilling to make peace in the valley. This is how many folks view Congress today, as two warring camps generating much heat and noise while accomplishing little.

Legislating Versus Governing

Let us assume that things will not change or improve significantly in the near term, and that the political culture of Congress will remain fixed on winning elections as opposed to national problem solving and lawmaking. So far, it has not resulted in an across the board, "throw the bums out" revolt at the polls. The closest public disgust has come to overturning the entire table in Congress is when there is an occasional change in party control in one house or the other.

What if a new dynamic or challenge was injected into the mix that might change Congress's approach to its role? No, I am not talking about abolishing congressional elections so that Congress will have more important things to worry about. This book is subtitled *From Fair Play to Power Plays*, which alludes to the current hyperpartisan Congress. This chapter, "Governing in a Political World," holds out the prospect of something other than hyperpartisan legislating as the governing model.

What if Congress could be convinced that its legislative role is not the most important thing it can do—and, in fact, that it is failing pretty miserably at it anyway? What if, as an alternative, Congress could be convinced that it could, alongside the president, play the more important role of actually governing the nation? What if this new approach could easily be carried out without changing congressional rules or circumventing the Constitution?

This may sound like semantic trickery. After all, is legislating not simply a part of governing—making the laws that authorize the executive branch to execute policy solutions that will govern the nation? Yes, legislating is part of governing—but just one small part. As Woodrow Wilson explained in his 1885 treatise *Congressional Government*, "Congress is fast becoming the governing body of the nation, and yet the only power which it possesses in perfection is the power which is but a part of government, the power of legislation." He goes on to explain that "legislation is but the oil of government. . . . It directs, it admonishes, but it does not do the actual heavy work of governing, . . . because it stands altogether apart from that work which it is set to see well done."[1]

And perhaps this is why Congress seems to dislike legislating so much: It is small ball that has been transformed into partisan dodge ball. As Congress has evolved over the last several decades from a culture of lawmaking to a culture of campaigning, its legislation has turned into partisan campaign tracts and bumper stickers.

When major legislation is brought up in a committee of Congress, it is almost accepted now that there will be strong party positions on it. Minority party amendments will be routinely rejected, and majority amendments will usually be adopted. There is little or no debate or discussion on the merits of the bill itself, and amendments are usually summarized perfunctorily before a nearly empty room. This is because committee rules in the House now allow the votes on amendments to be bundled and cast, one after another, at the end of the meeting. Only one-third of the committee members need to be present to cast votes on amendments, and only a majority for reporting out the bill to the House.

This process is repeated on the House and Senate floors, where most amendments and final-passage votes are cast along party lines. During general debate and debates on amendments, only a handful of members are in attendance on the floor until votes are called for. Members who may have some interest can monitor debates on television sets in their offices. Most just stay away and tend to other business.

Members are not unlike their constituents, who would be puzzled or bored by getting into the weeds of legislative legalese. As Wilson notes in his 1885 treatise, "Public opinion cannot be instructed or elevated by the debates of Congress, not only because there are few debates seriously undertaken by Congress, but principally because no one not professionally interested in the daily course of legislation cares to read what is said by the debaters." Wilson adds that "the ordinary citizen cannot be induced to pay much heed to the details or even to the main principles of lawmaking unless something more interesting than the law itself be involved in the pending decision," such as when "the fortunes of a party or the power of a great political leader are staked upon the final vote."[2]

When members of Congress are called to the floor for such a vote, they barely have time during the fifteen-minute vote to read the preprinted whip summaries of the bill or amendments before having to insert their voting cards in the electronic voting boxes along the aisle and push the "aye" or "nay" button. And subsequent votes in a bundled series are given only five minutes. After final passage of such a bill, the majority party prides itself on another win, and the minority party tries to put the worst face on the legislation, which will be used by its candidates against their opponents as campaign fodder in the next election campaign.

When Republicans retook control of the House in 2011, Speaker John Boehner vowed that he would restore the committee process and House floor debates so that members would feel they were not just "voting machines." However, this promise, which was also made by his predecessor (Pelosi) and successor (Ryan), always seems to fall short of the mark.

Boehner's voting machine metaphor for members is so apt that even members have come to think that this is their only real responsibility in Congress anymore. It is not unusual for them to complain about being dragged back to Washington on Mondays for possible votes after 6:30 P.M. on minor suspension bills. They complain that they resent having to return when nothing consequential is to be voted on. They miss the point that these Monday "bed check votes" are held to ensure that committees can begin conducting their business on Tuesday mornings.

On those weeks when the House does not begin voting until Tuesday evenings, quite often only Wednesdays and Thursdays are left for committee hearings and meetings if the House is not going to be in session on Friday. Is it any wonder that members find so little satisfaction or reward in the legislative process if they think the only thing really expected of them by their leaders is to cast votes in their committee and on the floor?

The following case study of Republican efforts to repeal and replace Obamacare in 2017 is illustrative of the state of governing and lawmaking in the early twenty-first century and of how power plays undermine deliberative policymaking.

Obamacare Versus Trumpcare

Ever since the Affordable Care Act, popularly known as Obamacare, was enacted in 2010, congressional Republicans have repeatedly touted the narrative that it was a policy doomed to failure because it was rammed through Congress in the dead of night with no one knowing what was in it, let alone how it could be successfully implemented. Chapter 3 described the process for passing Obamacare, which stretched over a period of fifteen months, had open committee hearings and amendments, and included public debate over the measure's merits. It was when things got down to the wire and leaders were scrambling to assemble sufficient votes to pass the bill that the process became more secretive, complex, and confusing.

When Republicans set out to repeal and replace Obamacare under unified party government at the beginning of the 115th Congress, their accelerated pace made the Democratic health care effort in the 111th Congress look like the quintessence of democratic deliberation. Congressional Republicans and their newly installed president, Donald J. Trump, had promised to make repealing and replacing Obamacare a top priority, and that became an urgent necessity for two reasons—one political and the other budget-driven.

First, candidate Trump raised unrealistic expectations during the campaign that a health care replacement bill could somehow be enacted almost immediately when he became president. In a campaign rally in suburban Philadelphia a week before the election, Trump vowed that he would "convene a special session" of Congress as soon as he was sworn in (never mind that Congress would have already been in session for seventeen days at that point) so Congress could "immediately repeal and replace Obamacare." For emphasis, he added that all this would happen "very, very quickly."[3]

128

Second, Republicans concluded they had to consider the health care measure under the budget act's reconciliation process by first adopting a budget resolution—a prerequisite for triggering reconciliation—even though Congress had not yet adopted a budget resolution for fiscal year 2017. As explained in chapter 3, reconciliation is the same path Democrats eventually chose to take in 2010 to complete action on Obamacare because the process requires only a majority vote in the Senate to pass the bill, as opposed to the sixty-vote majority needed to end filibusters.

From the day the 115th Congress convened on January 3, 2017, both houses moved swiftly to adopt a budget resolution, even though it meant circumventing formal Budget Committee consideration. The final budget resolution adopted on January 13 (S. Con. Res. 3) contained reconciliation instructions directing two committees in each house to produce legislation by January 27 that would reduce the deficit "by not less than" $1 billion during fiscal years 2017 to 2026.[4]

The four committees—the House Ways and Means Committee; House Energy and Commerce Committee; Senate Finance Committee; and Senate Health, Education, Labor, and Pensions Committee—dutifully met and performed their assigned tasks. The two House committees even pulled publicly televised all-nighters to debate, amend, and report their bills on time. Under the budget act, the committees must send their recommendations to their budget committees, which in turn must bundle them into a single bill and report them to their respective houses, without change.

However, under the terms of the budget act, the House Rules Committee can make in order additional amendments to make up for any shortfalls in the savings required. Moreover, the Rules Committee can make in order other amendments that may be necessary for political purposes, such as to secure a majority vote for passage, although this purpose is not mentioned in the budget act. It was to this latter end that between March 23 and May 4 three special rules for reconciliation were presented to the House in the quest to push the reconciliation bill across the finish line and send it to the Senate. What made the going so rough, in part, were the bad news cost estimates from the Congressional Budget Office on the various iterations of the bill. The office predicted that more than twenty million insured Americans would lose their existing coverage by 2020 if Trumpcare replaced Obamacare, and their premiums would increase by 50 percent.[5]

These prospects set off noisy outcries and protest rallies across the nation against tampering with or repealing Obamacare. It was almost a mirror image of the Tea Party rebellion in 2010 against the Democrats who supported Obamacare. Much of the town hall furor to shout down members of Congress was part of the larger Democratic "resist" movement to oppose every move of the Trump administration, but some Trump voters were also in the audiences, and they were deeply upset about their possible loss of Obamacare coverage.

The Republican health care alternatives being batted around Congress did not begin to match the promises candidate Trump had made about what his replacement bill would contain—which included making health insurance available to everybody; reducing health care costs; not cutting Medicaid; ensuring that no one would lose coverage; making insurance available across state lines; and ensuring that no one would be worse off financially. The GOP Obamacare replacement bill reported in Congress failed on all six counts.[6] Nevertheless, the president was willing to defer to the legislative drafters in Congress rather than attempt to draft his own bill in the White House that would somehow fulfill all his campaign promises.

Because the Rules Committee did not solicit amendments from members, as it does when it is contemplating a so-called structured rule, the assumption was that the bill would be considered under a closed amendment rule. Nevertheless, thirty-one amendments were filed with the committee, twenty-seven by Republicans and four by Democrats. The large number of Republican amendments was a tipoff to the leadership that the bill was already in trouble if brought to the floor as reported from the Budget Committee.

After some delay, a reconciliation rule (H. Res. 228) was reported to the House on March 24. It provided for four hours of general debate and self-executed the adoption of six amendments printed in the report on the rule—four by the chairpersons of the two committees that reported reconciliation recommendations, and two others designed to attract support from Republican Freedom Caucus members.

Not surprisingly, the summary of the six-part, self-executing provisions in the rule read like the assembly instructions for the kind of child's doll house that drive dads mad on Christmas Day: "The resolution provides that the amendment printed in part A of this report, modified by the amendment printed in part B of this report shall be considered as adopted"; and "the amendment printed in part C of this report, modified by the amendments printed in part D and part E of this report, shall be considered as adopted."[7]

Shortly after the House convened at 10 A.M. on Friday, March 24, the Rules Committee chairman, Pete Sessions, filed the special rule on the health care bill and then immediately called it up for consideration. After the usual hour of debate on the rule, it was adopted, 230–194.

Following some unrelated procedural votes, the health care bill was called up at about 11:15 A.M. by Representative Diane Black (R-TN), chairwoman of the Budget Committee. After general debate, the speaker pro tempore declared at 3:31 P.M. that "further consideration of HR 1628 is postponed," and then promptly gaveled the House into recess.[8] In the interim, before the House reconvened at 4:30 P.M., Speaker Ryan traveled to the White House to inform the president that he did not have the votes to pass the bill and to suggest that the bill be pulled. The president agreed.

Although some observers thought this was the death blow to repeal and replace, Republicans and the president saw it as an opportunity to reconnoiter. Two weeks later, on April 6, the Rules Committee reported yet another special rule (H. Res. 254), with yet another self-executing amendment. But a whip count revealed that the addition would still not make the difference, and the rule was not even brought up on the floor.

Once again, death notices were prematurely circulated. On May 4, a third rule (H. Res. 308) was brought to the floor, this time containing two self-executing amendments worked out by a representative each from the Freedom Caucus and the moderate Tuesday Group of Republicans. The bill (as automatically amended) narrowly passed the House, 217–213, with 217 Republicans voting in the affirmative and just 20 voting against. The House had finally shaken the bill loose from internal GOP conference gridlock and shipped the measure off to an uncertain fate in the Senate.

President Trump was so pleased by the House action that he bused the entire House Republican membership down to the White House for a celebration in the Rose Garden—something ordinarily reserved for bill-signing ceremonies. Despite the celebration, Trump would later characterize the House-passed bill as "mean"—an indicator of his mercurial temperament.[9]

In the Senate, Majority Leader Mitch McConnell did not have the advantage of a Rules Committee, with its arsenal of closed and self-executing rules. All he needed, however, was the right formula to get to 50 votes (from his 52-member caucus), plus the tie-breaking vote of Vice President Mike Pence, if needed. But that would prove difficult to achieve. McConnell narrowly cleared the first hurdle on the motion to proceed to the consideration of the bill on July 25, 51–50.

Over the next five days, the Senate considered a small number of Republican amendments and several Democratic procedural motions (for example, to "recommit"). Finally, on July 28, the scheduled get-away day for the August recess, a last ditch vote was taken on a so-called skinny repeal amendment. It failed, 49–51, with three Republicans voting no: senators Susan Collins (ME), John McCain (AZ), and Lisa Murkowski (AK). The president was furious over the three Republican defectors, and also with Senate Majority Leader McConnell, whom he continued to verbally pummel during the August recess.

Once again, the bill was left for dead. However, it enjoyed a brief resurrection two weeks before the curtain fell on fiscal year 2017 on September 30, and with it expiration of the majority vote treatment for the reconciliation bill in the Senate. On September 18, Republican senators Lindsey Graham (SC) and Bill Cassidy (LA) unveiled a new alternative that would block-grant the Obamacare subsidies and Medicaid expansion monies to the states in 2020 and leave it to them to devise their own health care options.

Senator John McCain—who had cast the decisive, thumbs-down no vote on July 28—continued to insist in the interim that he would not vote for a bill that had not been vetted through the regular order of the committee process. He held to this standard and announced on Friday, September 22, that he would oppose Graham-Cassidy under current conditions: "I would consider supporting legislation similar to that offered by my friends Senators Graham and Cassidy were it the product of extensive hearings, debate, and amendment. But that has not been the case."[10]

Ironically, Lamar Alexander (TN)—chairman of the Senate Health, Education, Labor, and Pensions Committee—and the committee's ranking Democrat, Patty Murray (WA), had been working since late July in their committee on a bipartisan health care compromise to guarantee the Obamacare subsidies for at least another year in return for giving states more flexibility in how they implemented the insurance rules. However, Alexander suspended the effort on September 19 when ensnared in the simultaneous pincer move of Graham-Cassidy from the right and

Senator Bernie Sanders's Medicare-for-all bill from the left (with fifteen Democratic cosponsors).[11]

The reconciliation resurrection was short-lived. In addition to Senator McCain holding firm in opposition, the two other Republican opponents from late July, senators Collins and Murkowski, refused to be bought off by a revised version promising more money for their states. Additionally, Senator Rand Paul (KY) joined in opposition because Graham-Cassidy simply shifted the same amount of federal monies to another pocket.

Majority Leader McConnell cleverly promised only to "consider" Graham-Cassidy, and did not commit to a vote on it without knowing where the votes were. Emerging from the Tuesday, September 26, GOP policy lunch, McConnell announced that he was pulling the plug on reconciliation for lack of votes. But he vowed that the repeal-and-replace effort would be revisited at some later date.[12]

The Republican quest to repeal and replace Obamacare came to yet another sorry end, despite more than sixty repeal votes cast over seven years. Unlike the earlier votes taken while Obama was still president, this time members were playing with real bullets under unified party government, and thus they would need to accept full responsibility and accountability for the results.

The decision to rush something through early in the 115th Congress (although stretched out over nine months of fits and starts) was at odds with the need to act in a responsible and deliberative manner. Contrasted with President Obama's fifteen-month effort, in which he first sought buy-in from all the affected parties before pushing Congress to act, Republicans had not bothered to consult with any of the numerous stakeholders—from doctors, nurses, patients, and hospitals to insurance firms, drug companies, and employers providing employees with coverage.

Overall, it was a slap-dash, confusing rush to the finish line, with many of the runners not fully comprehending what the race was all about or where that finish line was. Consequently, what

Republicans came up with did not hold up as a viable policy alternative that could inspire public credibility and confidence. That was clear from poll after poll showing that Obamacare was far more popular than any of the GOP variations. For instance, a *Washington Post*–ABC News poll released on September 23 found that 56 percent of the public preferred Obamacare, versus just 33 percent who favored the Graham-Cassidy alternative.[13]

Although repeal and replace may have been a long-standing political high priority for Republicans, the way in which it was handled did not bode well for the party, regardless of whether it passed or failed. The bottom line, for the purposes of this book, is that power plays cannot succeed in the long run if they are not utilized in the furtherance of sound, publicly supported policies.

Big Picture Governing

Although one might hope that a new era of bipartisan governance will slowly dawn as a result of the president's setback on health care and the seeming intractability of the House Freedom Caucus, the other side of the coin is that Democrats have vowed unyielding resistance to and noncooperation with anything with the "Trump" brand on it. Their attitude is not dissimilar to Republican leader Mitch McConnell's vow in 2010 to do everything he could to make sure Obama would be "a one-term president."

Obviously, that approach did not work out, although Obamacare was probably the main reason Republicans regained control of the House in 2010. It may also have been a factor in the GOP winning back the Senate in 2014. And it certainly was a major campaign pledge in Trump's winning presidential bid in 2016. Lines in the sand have been drawn that will not be easy to erase with wishful thinking. A return to bipartisanship may not be "utopian," but it is unlikely to happen in the immediate future, except on smaller issues that do not excite either party's base.

But what about the other type of governing that Woodrow Wilson had in mind when he wrote that Congress should place a higher value on governing than on legislating? He was no utopian (although many considered him an idealist), and he certainly was enamored of the Westminster governing model and the importance of parliamentary debates. Did he have in mind somehow transplanting a parliamentary system to replace what he considered the outmoded American constitutional system, with its bulky checks and balances?

Without fully fleshing out Wilson's ever-changing ideas of how the US system might be transformed constitutionally, I confine the remaining discussion to how he envisioned Congress in a larger, governing capacity, not replacing the president and executive branch but sharing in directing executive departments and agencies. Whatever the intention was behind "the compromises of Constitution-making in 1787," wrote Wilson, "the result was to give us, not government by discussion, . . . but only legislation by discussion, which is no more than a small part of government by discussion." Government by discussion, Wilson went on, is "debate of all matters of administration." It is "the proper duty of a representative body to look diligently into every affair of government." Unless Congress uses every means to scrutinize the acts of administrative agents, he wrote, "the country must be helpless to learn how it is being served . . . [and] remain in embarrassing, crippling ignorance of the very affairs which is most important that it should understand and direct." Here, Wilson again compares the importance of this role with legislating: "The informing function of Congress should be preferred even to its legislative function," because such talk, "when earnestly and purposefully conducted, clears the public mind and shapes the demands of public opinion."[14]

However, he was not suggesting that Congress should choose government by discussion over legislation by discussion. Instead, he was prioritizing one over the other by saying that Congress's

"legislative purposes might be most fortunately clarified and sim-
plified," if first squared "by a conscientious attention to the par-
amount and controlling duty of understanding, discussing, and
directing administration." Put another way, oversight of government must precede legislating if the legislation is to address the
real problems and needs that come to light.[15] The problem is,
Congress is not inclined to engage in oversight unless something
sensational or scandalous turns up. That is when numerous committees and subcommittees jump into the act to hold duplicative
investigative oversight hearings—vying to bathe in the broad light
of klieg lamps.

Nevertheless, it is my contention that Wilson was onto something worth serious consideration, and this is the notion of a larger
governing purpose Congress could fulfill to improve the standing
of government generally, and of Congress in particular. It can
be done by highlighting the importance of Congress's informing
function in enhancing the public's understanding of the operations of its government.[16]

All this is premised, of course, on the assumptions that Congress is capable of and interested in performing this larger governing role—what I refer to as "big picture governing" in contrast
to small picture legislating. The one thing that may make this
approach more attractive is recognizing the clear link between the
public discussions of government performance and its immediate
by-product: more thoughtful and effective legislative solutions.
Presumably, such a two-step process could lead to more bipartisan, consensus-based solutions if members take the time to work
through competing explanations and reason together about the
nature of a problem and its alternative solutions (a definition of
"deliberation" used in my previous book).

"Taking the time" to do what is needed is the essence of what
is required—and what Congress is currently unwilling to do. As
Wilson recognized, "It is not surprising . . . that the enacting,
revising, tinkering, repealing of laws should engross the attention

and engage the entire energy of such a body as Congress."[17] By first looking at the big picture, getting all the facts straight, and working across the aisle on a problem, Congress will later be saving itself wasted time on the minutiae of tinkering with, revising, and repealing bad laws.

Ironically, this is how early Congresses approached problem solving and legislation; the House would first hold a general debate on a problem and options for solving it in the Committee of the Whole (comprising all House members), and it would then appoint and direct a select committee to draft the legislative solution.

There are myriad recommendations around Washington for improving Congress's use of time and its performance. The Bipartisan Policy Center's Commission on Political Reform (on which I served as an adviser) issued a series of recommendations in 2014 that included proposals to allow more time for Congress to do its oversight and legislative work.

Among other things, the Commission on Political Reform called on Congress to institute five-day workweeks, with three weeks on followed by one week off; to adopt biennial budgeting for budget resolutions and appropriations bills, thereby freeing up one year for more oversight activities and authorizing legislation; and to ensure that committee chairpersons consult in advance with the minority party on their ideas before rushing to markup on the chairperson's mark, to make possible some minority party buy-in at the outset.[18] I would add the recommendation that the House remove the three-term limits on House committee chairs to further empower committees and enhance their continuity in expertise.

House committees are already required by rules to adopt their legislative and oversight agendas at the beginning of each Congress, coordinate these with the leadership and with the House Oversight and Government Reform Committee, publish their plans, and account for their accomplishments at the end of the Congress in their final activity reports. There is no question that such oversight and legislative plans, if implemented and publicly reported on, can lead to greater public discussion and awareness of the federal government branches' operations.

Wilson felt strongly that the informing function should not be left entirely to the press: "One of our chief constitutional difficulties," he wrote, "is that, in opportunities for informing and guiding public opinion, the freedom of the press is greater than the freedom of Congress. . . . Congress is altogether excluded from the arrangement by which the press declares what the executive is, and conventions of the national parties decide what the executive shall be."[19]

What Wilson did hope for, over and above governing by legislation (and parties), was for big picture governing, whereby Congress first sorts out the nature of our problems on the ground and how our government is dealing with them, and then informs the people of its findings. In so doing, Wilson felt, Congress could help shape public opinion to favor ameliorative government actions that will be widely accepted and effective. It is not unrealistic to think that such big picture governing might eventually attract strong bipartisan support, both among the people and within Congress.

Appendix

Table A.1

Special Rules Providing for the Original Consideration of Legislation in the House of Representatives, 103rd–114th Congresses

Congress	Open / Modified Open		Structured		Closed		Totals	
	Number	Percent	Number	Percent	Number	Percent	Number	Percent
103rd (1993–94)	46	44%	49	47%	9	9%	104	100%
104th (1995–96)	83	58%	40	28%	19	14%	142	100%
105th (1997–98)	74	53%	42	30%	24	17%	140	100%
106th (1999–2000)	91	51%	49	27%	39	22%	179	100%
107th (2001–2)	40	37%	44	41%	23	22%	107	100%
108th (2003–4)	34	26%	62	47%	37	28%	133	101%
109th (2005–6)	24	19%	61	49%	40	32%	125	100%
110th (2007–8)	23	14%	81	50%	59	36%	163	100%
111th (2009–10)	0	0%	73	65%	38	34%	111	100%
112th (2011–12)	25	18%	65	46%	50	36%	140	100%
113th (2013–14)	12	8%	65	43%	72	48%	149	99%
114th (2015–16)	8	5%	82	53%	65	42%	155	100%

Note: The table applies only to special rules providing for the initial consideration for amendment of bills, joint resolutions, and significant concurrent resolutions (for example, budget, war-related). It does not apply to privileged resolutions considered in the House, to subsequent rules for the same measure, to conference reports, or to special rules that only waive points of order against appropriations bills but do not provide for consideration in the Committee of the Whole. Rules making in order more than one bill are counted as a separate rule for each measure made in order; for example, a rule providing for the consideration of four bills under closed rules is counted as four closed rules. An open rule is one that permits any member to offer an amendment otherwise germane in the Committee of the Whole under the five-minute rule. A modified open rule is one that either requires the preprinting of amendments in the *Congressional Record*, sets an overall time cap on the amendment process, or both. A structured rule is one that limits the amendments that can be offered to those specified in the special rule and/or report on the rule (and now includes previously designated modified closed rules that allowed just one amendment). A closed rule is one that permits the offering of no amendments (except those recommended by the reporting committee(s).

Sources: Committee on Rules and personal examination of texts of and reports on special rules reported by the House Rules Committee. Compiled by Don Wolfensberger, resident scholar, Bipartisan Policy Center.

Table A.2
Self-Executing Rules, 101st–114th Congresses

Congress	Total Rules	Self-Executing Rules	As Percentage of Total
101st (1989–90)	90	16	18%
102nd (1991–92)	150	26	17%
103rd (1993–94)	135	30	22%
104th (1995–96)	151	38	25%
105th (1997–98)	147	52	35%
106th (1999–2000)	184	38	21%
107th (2001–2)	115	41	36%
108th (2003–4)	139	30	22%
109th (2005–6)	125	29	23%
110th (2007–8)	162	52	32%
111th (2009–10)	111	45	41%
112th (2011–12)	141	36	26%
113th (2013–14)	149	55	37%
114th (2015–16)	155	47	30%

Note: A self-executing rule is a simple House resolution reported by the Rules Committee providing for the consideration of a bill or joint resolution that also provides for the adoption of an amendment to the bill or joint resolution upon adoption of the special rule (that is, the specified amendment is automatically adopted before the bill is even taken up). For example, the special rule will often read, "The amendment in the nature of a substitute recommended by the Committee on __ now printed in the bill, *modified by the amendment printed in Part A of the report of the Committee on Rules accompanying this resolution, shall be considered as adopted.*"

Appendix

Table A.3

Self-Executing Rules for Committee Amendments Versus New Amendments, 101st–114th Congresses

Congress	Committee Amendments	Committee Amendments as Percentage of Total	New Amendments	New Amendments as Percentage of Total	Total Self-Executing Rules
101st (1989–90)	2	13%	14	87%	16
102nd (1991–92)	4	15%	22	85%	26
103rd (1993–94)	4	13%	26	87%	30
104th (1995–96)	4	11%	34	89%	38
105th (1997–98)	12	23%	40	77%	52
106th (1999–2000)	11	29%	27	71%	38
107th (2001–2)	13	32%	28	69%	41
108th (2003–4)	10	33%	20	67%	30
109th (2005–6)	8	28%	21	72%	29
110th (2007–8)	14	27%	38	73%	52
111th (2009–10)	15	33%	30	67%	45
112th (2011–12)	8	22%	28	78%	36
113th (2013–14)	17	31%	38	69%	55
114th (2015–16)	17	36%	30	64%	47

Note: A self-executing provision in a special rule is one that provides for the automatic adoption of additional language into the legislation upon the adoption of the rule. The total number of rules used for self-executing rules is sometimes greater than the total used for amendment type rules because it includes not only rules for initial consideration of bills and joint resolution but for simple and concurrent resolution and for adopting Senate amendments to House bills.

Table A.4

Amendments Made in Order by Party Sponsor in Structured Rules Reported
by the House Rules Committee (111th–114th Congresses, 2009–2016)

Amendments	111th Congress (2009–10)— Democratic Majority	112th Congress (2011–12)— Republican Majority	113th Congress (2013–14)— Republican Majority*	114th Congress (2015–16)— Republican Majority
Democratic amendments: Number (and percentage of total)	551 (62%)	493 (60%)	446 (47%)	554 (45%)
Republican amendments: Number (and percentage of total)	336 (38%)	279 (34%)	374 (39%)	486 (39%)
Bipartisan amendments: Number (and percentage of total)	N.A.	52 (6%)	132 (14%)	193 (16%)
Total amendments	887	824	952	1,233
Total structured rules	73	65	65	82
Average amendments per structured rule	12.2	12.7	14.6	15
Total rules	111	140	149	155
Structured rules as percentage of total rules	66%	46%	44%	53%
Open rules: Number (and percentage of total rules)	0 (0%)	25 (18%)	12 (8%)	8 (5%)
Closed rules: Number and percentage of total rules)	38 (34%)	50 (36%)	72 (48%)	65 (42%)

Note: The amendments listed above do not include those offered under open rules in the 112th Congress and 113th Congress (primarily on appropriations bills). Data were extracted from special rule tables maintained by Don Wolfensberger of the Bipartisan Policy Center, based on inspections of individual rules and committee reports and summaries on them. Structured rules include all those special rules reported by the Rules Committee that specify the amendments that can be offered (and include modified closed rules that only allow for one minority amendment). Open rules here include modified open rules that may impose a time cap on the amendment process and/or require preprinting of amendments in the *Congressional Record* but otherwise do not restrict or specify what amendments may be offered (as long as they otherwise comport with House rules). Beginning in the 112th Congress, under the House Republican majority, certain amendments were designated as bipartisan by the Rules Committee at the request of their authors. N.A. means not available.

Appendix

Table A.5

Comparative Data on Unreported Measures on Which Special Rules Were Granted in the House of Representatives, 109th–114th Congresses

Measure	109th Congress (2005–6)	110th Congress (2007–8)	111th Congress (2009–10)	112th Congress (2011–12)	113th Congress (2013–14)	114th Congress (2015–16)
Total measures with special rules	125	163	111	140	149	155
Unreported measures with special rules	34	35	29	38	55	39
Unreported measures as percentage of total	27%	21%	26%	27%	37%	25%
Unreported measures with closed rules	28	32	21	31	47	35
Total closed rules	40	59	38	50	72	65
Unreported closed as percentage of all closed	70%	54%	55%	62%	65%	54%

Source: Compiled by Don Wolfensberger of the Bipartisan Policy Center, from an examination of special rules on the Rules Committee's website.

Notes

Introduction

1. Newt Gingrich, *Lessons Learned the Hard Way: A Personal Report* (New York: HarperCollins, 1998), 166–67.

2. Ron Elving, "CQ Roundtable: The Revolution at Twilight," *Congressional Quarterly Weekly Report*, April 4, 1998, 198.

3. H. Res. 385, 114th Congress, 1st Session, introduced July 28, 2015.

4. "Remarks of Hon. Paul Ryan," *Congressional Record*, October 29, 2015, H7339.

5. Sheryl Gay Stolberg and Nicholas Fandos, "In Congress, Only Gloom Is Bipartisan," *New York Times*, January 28, 2018.

1. Rolling Rules

1. Thomas Jefferson, *A Manual of Parliamentary Practice for the Use of the Senate of the United States* (Washington: US Government Printing Office, 1993; first published 1801), 2. Jefferson compiled the manual while serving as vice president of the United States and thus the presiding officer of the Senate (1797–1801).

2. Thomas B. Reed, "Rules of the House of Representatives," *Century Magazine* 36, no. 106 (April 1888–April 1889): 795.

3. US Constitution, Article I, sec. 5, clause 3.

4. Alexander Hamilton, James Madison, and John Jay, *The Federalist Papers*, No. 10 (New York: Mentor Books, 1961), 71.

5. Greg Weiner, *Madison's Metronome: The Constitution, Majority Rule, and the Tempo of American Politics* (Lawrence: University Press of Kansas, 2012), 72–79.

6. Hamilton, Madison, and Jay, *Federalist* No. 10, 82.

7. Jefferson, *A Manual of Parliamentary Practice*, xxix.

8. Jefferson, 1.

9. DeAlva Stanwood Alexander, *History and Procedure of the House of Representatives* (Charleston, S.C.: BiblioLife, 2009; first published by Houghton Mifflin, 1916), 180.

10. US Congress, *A History of the Committee on Rules, 1st to 97th Congress, 1789–1981* (Washington, D.C.: US Government Printing Office, 1983), Rules Committee Print (Ninety-seventh Cong., 2nd Session), 34–38.

11. *Annals of Congress*, April 7, 1789, 98–102; and April 13, 1789, 121–22.

12. James Madison, letter to Edmund Randolph, May 31, 1789, in *The Papers of James Madison*, vol. 12, ed. Charles F. Hobson and Robert A. Rutland (Charlottesville: University Press of Virginia, 1979), 189–90.

13. See the discussion by Donald R. Wolfensberger, *Congress and the People: Deliberative Democracy on Trial* (Washington, D.C., and Baltimore, Md.: Woodrow Wilson Center Press and Johns Hopkins University Press, 2000), chap. 2, "The Bill of Rights: Madison Gets Religion," 21–40.

14. Sarah Binder, *Minority Rights, Majority Rule* (Cambridge: Cambridge University Press, 1997).

15. Alexander, *History and Procedure*, 181.

16. Binder, *Minority Right, Majority Rule*, 29, 65–67.

17. Alexander, *History and Procedure*, 187–90.

18. Binder, *Minority Rights, Majority Rule*, 8–11.

19. Alexander, *History and Procedure*, 184.

20. US Congress, *History of the Committee on Rules*, 49–51.

21. Alexander, *History and Procedure*, 196. *Riders* are legislative provisions tacked onto appropriations bills; *disappearing quorums* occur when members do not answer to their names during a quorum call even though present in the chamber.

22. US Congress, *History of the Committee on Rules*, 61–62.

23. US Congress, 63.

24. Alexander, *History and Procedure*, 191. The first instance occurred in 1841, when the Select Committee on Rules issued a report that allowed

for a suspension of the rules by majority (instead of a two-thirds) vote to dislodge a matter from the Committee of the Whole, where it was being filibustered, and bring the matter to a final vote in the House without further amendment.

25. James Grant, Mr. *Speaker: The Life and Times of Thomas B. Reed, the Man Who Broke the Filibuster* (New York: Simon & Schuster, 2011), 260.

26. US Congress, *History of the United States House of Representatives, 1789–1994* (Washington, D.C.: US Government Printing Office, 1994), House Document 103–324 (103rd Cong., 2nd Session), 182.

27. US Congress, *History of the Committee on Rules*, 72–73.

28. US Congress, 74–75.

29. Grant, *Mr. Speaker*, 288–89.

30. Jefferson, *A Manual of Parliamentary Practice*.

31. Donald R. Wolfensberger, "Adopting House Rules in a New Congress: From Democratic Deliberation to Partisan Monopoly," *Congressional Record*, January 7, 1997, 14–16 et seq.; also published in a modified form by Woodrow Wilson Center, January 4, 2007, and updated August 2014, www.wilsoncener.org/sites/default/files;rulesadoptionpaper.pdf.

2. Making House Rules

1. Dingell was beginning his twenty-seventh term in Congress, having been first elected in 1954 to succeed his father. Pelosi was the ninth speaker he served under, dating back to Speaker Sam Rayburn. Dingell retired eight years later, in 2014, after one more swearing-in of Pelosi as speaker, and twice swearing in the tenth and final speaker he would serve under, Representative John Boehner of Ohio. Dingell was succeeded in his Michigan congressional district by his wife, Representative Debbie Dingell, carrying on the "all in the family" tradition.

2. Ordinarily, adoption of rules at the beginning of a Congress is handled in a single resolution (House Resolution 5), debatable for one hour and followed by an up-or-down vote on the entire package unless the minority succeeds on a procedural vote to recommit the resolution to a select committee with instructions to immediately report back specified amendments. House Resolution 5 provided, instead, for a process for considering House Resolution 6, adopting rules for the 110th Congress, which allowed for a separate debate and vote on each of the five titles of House Resolution 6 and permitted one motion to recommit the package to a select committee,

with or without instructions (the minority party prerogative to offer its rules alternatives).

3. Remarks of the Honorable Louise Slaughter, *Congressional Record,* January 4, 2007, H8–9.

4. "Honest Leadership and Open Government Act of 2006," HR 4682, introduced by Representative Nancy Pelosi on February 1, 2006, along with 162 cosponsors; and S. 2180, introduced by Senator Harry Reid, February 1, 2006, with 40 cosponsors.

5. "A New Direction for America," *Washington Post,* September 19, 2015, www.washingtonpost.com/wp-sv/special/politics/politial-rallying-cry /new-direcion-for-america.pdf.

6. For a more detailed description of the Republicans' contract exercise, see Donald R. Wolfensberger, *Congress and the People: Deliberative Democracy on Trial* (Washington, D.C. and Baltimore, Md.: Woodrow Wilson Center Press and Johns Hopkins University Press, 2000), chap. 10, "The Road to the Republican Revolution," and chap. 11, "The Road to Governance: Revolution, Reform and Reality," 175–91.

7. "Summary of House Rules Package [House Resolution 6], Opening Day of the 110th Congress, Prepared by the Rules Committee, Louise M. Slaughter, Chairwoman-Designate," *Congressional Record,* January 4, 2007, H7–8.

8. House Resolution 6, *Congressional Record,* January 4, 2007, H19–23.

9. Remarks of the Honorable David Dreier, *Congressional Record,* January 4, 2007, H9–10.

10. The Republican majority in the 104th Congress had also employed a two-step rules adoption process, the first of its kind process through two resolutions, House Resolution 5 and House Resolution 6, to allow for separate debates and votes on various sections of the package. Most of the changes were adopted by overwhelming bipartisan majorities. The special rule for the Congressional Accountability Act, however, was adopted on a party-line vote, even though the bill itself was subsequently passed, 429–0.

11. "New House Principles: A Congress for All Americans," Office of the House Democratic Leader Nancy Pelosi, May 25, 2006, www.Democratic Leader.house.gov.

12. "Text of Amendment to H. Res. 5, offered by Mr. Dreier of California, Mr. McHenry of North Carolina, and Mr. Price of Georgia," *Congressional Record,* January 4, 2007, H16; previous question vote (Roll No. 3), H16–17.

13. "Text of Amendment to H. Res. 5," H17–18. The minority party's motion to commit the opening day House rules package with amendatory instructions had fallen into disuse in the 1890s, when responsibility for

drafting the resolution had switched from the Rules Committee. It was only rediscovered in an obscure section of the multivolume set of House precedents in 1980, and put back into use in 1981.

14. *Congressional Record*, January 5, 2007, H83–84.

15. George B. Galloway, *History of the United States House of Representatives* (Washington. D.C.: US Government Printing Office, 1965), House Document 250 (Eighty-ninth Cong., 1st Session), 48.

16. Galloway, *History of the United States House of Representatives*, 48.

17. *Congressional Record*, January 5, 1981, House Resolution 5, adopting House Rules for the 101st Congress, motion to commit with instructions offered by Representative Robert H. Michel, 112–13. Republicans had discovered a precedent from 1893 in which the House was acting under general parliamentary law before its standing rules had been adopted and a motion to seat a new member was offered. When someone offered a substitute amendment, the previous question was moved on the resolution and substitute. Another member then offered a motion to commit the resolution to a select committee of five with instructions to report back in ten days. When a point of order was raised that the commit motion was not in order after the previous question had been moved, the speaker overruled the point of order on grounds that, under parliamentary law, the motion to commit was in order pending the demand for the previous question or after it is ordered. (*Hinds' Precedents*, vol. 5, sec. 5604). As it turned out, that precedent was later extended to opening day rules resolutions in the early part of the twentieth century, with minority Republicans and later minority Democrats using the motion to commit with instructions to report back "forthwith" with specified amendments. However, the practice was abandoned or forgotten by the late 1920s, and minorities came to rely solely on the previous question votes in an attempt to offer their substitute rules packages.

18. *Congressional Record*, March 15, 1909, H27–28.

19. *Congressional Record*, H21.

20. *Congressional Record*, H22.

21. *Congressional Record*, H23.

22. US Congress, *A History of the Committee on Rules, 1st to 97th Congress, 1789–1981* (Washington, D.C.: US Government Printing Office, 1983), Rules Committee Print (Ninety-seventh Cong., 2nd Session), 82–91.

23. *Congressional Record*, January 9, 1911, 679–87. Also see *Cannon's Precedents*, vol. 8, secs. 3376 and 3377, and Don Wolfensberger, "Czar Speaker Is Vindicated on Overthrow Ruling," *Roll Call*, January 15, 2014.

3. Procedural Triage for Health Care Reform

1. Remarks of the Honorable Nancy Pelosi, *Congressional Record*, January 6, 2009, H5.

2. Pelosi, through her caucus, had just replaced Dingell as chairman of the Energy and Commerce Committee with Representative Henry Waxman (CA), who was more sympathetic to tough clean air standards than the representative from the Motor City. Nevertheless, Dingell remained an active and engaged member of the committee and contributed greatly to the health care debate and legislative outcomes. Ironically, as chairman of the Energy and Commerce Committee in the 103rd Congress (1993–94), Dingell was unable to get his committee to report President Bill Clinton's major health care legislation.

3. "Remarks of President Barack Obama before a Joint Session of Congress," *Congressional Record*, September 9, 2009, H9391.

4. "Remarks by the President and Vice President at Signing of the Health Insurance Reform Bill," White House Transcript, March 30, 2010, www .whitehouse.gov/photos-and-video/video/president-obama-signs-health -reform-law#transcript.

5. *Congressional Quarterly Almanac: 103rd Congress, 1st Session–1993* (Washington, D.C.: Congressional Quarterly, 1994), vol. 49, 335.

6. Robert Pear, "Team Effort in the House to Overhaul Health Care," *New York Times*, March 18, 2009.

7. Henry Waxman with Joshua Green, *The Waxman Report: How Congress Really Works* (New York: Twelve, Hachette Book Group, 2009; epilogue, 2010), 230–32.

8. "Landmark Health Care Overhaul: A Long, Acrimonious Journey," *CQ Almanac, 2009* (Washington, D.C.: CQ–Roll Call Group, 2010), vol. 65, 13–3, 13–4.

9. Waxman, *Waxman Report*, 233.

10. "Landmark Health Care Overhaul," 13–4, 13–5, 13–8.

11. House Report 111–330, to accompany House Resolution 903, "Providing for consideration of the bill (HR 3962) to provide affordable quality health care for all Americans . . . and the bill (HR 3961) . . . to reform the Medicare SGR payment system for physicians." Because House Rules provide that a two-thirds vote is needed to consider a special rule on the same day it is filed, the House remained in session for the legislative day of November 6 so the rule could be considered on the next legislative day without a supermajority vote being required.

12. *Huffington Post*, November 9, 2009, quoted by Barbara Sinclair, *Unorthodox Lawmaking* (Washington, D.C.: CQ Press, 2012), 198.

13. David Clarke and Paul M. Krawzak, "Both Chambers Float Budget Plans," *CQ Weekly*, March 30, 2009, 725.

14. "Landmark Health Care Overhaul," 13–3 et seq.

15. Don Wolfensberger, "Slaughter Solution for Health Care Suffers Whiplash," Procedural Politics (column), *Roll Call*, March 23, 2010.

16. Sinclair, *Unorthodox Lawmaking*, 218.

17. Wolfensberger, "Slaughter Solution."

18. Wolfensberger.

19. "H. Res. 1203, providing for consideration of the Senate amendments to the bill (HR 3590) . . . [and] of the bill (HR 4872) to provide for reconciliation pursuant to . . . the concurrent resolution on the budget for fiscal year 2010"; and H. Rept. 111–448, a report of the Committee on Rules to accompany H. Res. 1203.

20. *Congressional Record*, March 21, 2010, H1824–28.

21. *Congressional Record*, H1828–33. The Senate-passed bill had a number of earmarks in return for senators' support. They became so notorious that they acquired nicknames, which Representative David Dreier recited at page H1835: the "Louisiana purchase," the "Cornhusker kickback," the "Bismarck bank job," and "Gator aid." If enacted, the reconciliation bill's "fixes" would self-execute the earmarks out of the Senate bill, removing a source of embarrassment for all.

22. *Congressional Record*, H1895.

23. *Congressional Record*, H1896.

24. *CQ Almanac, 2010* (Washington, D.C.: CQ–Roll Call Group, 2011), vol. 66, 9-3-9-13.

25. Public Law 111–152.

26. According to the Kaiser Health Tracking Poll in April 2016, only 38 percent of the American people have a favorable view of Obamacare, and 49 percent have an unfavorable view; accessed at http://kff.org/health-reform/report/kaiser-health-tracking-poll-april-2016/.

4. Fraying Purse Strings

1. CBS News, *Face the Nation*, September 27, 2015, www.cbsnews.com/news/face-the-nation-transcripts-september-27-boehner-sanders-kasich/.

2. House Resolution 385, 114th Congress, introduced by Representative Mark Meadows, July 28, 2015. Meadows, a small business owner from Jackson County, N.C., was first elected to the House in 2012. He introduced the resolution on his fifty-sixth birthday. A similar resolution was offered

unsuccessfully by a Democrat in 1910 to remove Republican House Speaker Joe Cannon of Illinois. In 2016, Meadows was elected chairman of the Freedom Caucus for the 115th Congress.

3. House Resolution 385. The preamble disqualified the resolution as privileged, although an alternative with only the resolving clause could be called up on the floor at any time and offered repeatedly.

4. Bob Woodward, *The Price of Politics* (New York: Simon & Shuster, 2012), 326. Obama would later claim during a presidential debate with Mitt Romney in 2012, "The sequester is not something that I've proposed. It is something that Congress has proposed"—a claim ruled "mostly false" by Politi-Fact, October 24, 2012, www.politifact.com/truth-o-meter/statements/2012/oct/24/barack-obama/obama-says-congress-owns-sequestration-cuts/.

5. CBS News, *Face the Nation.*

6. "Boehner's Last Deal," *CQ Weekly*, November 2, 2015, 7–8.

7. Tamar Hallerman, "Barn Is Cleared for the New Speaker," *CQ Weekly*, November 2, 2015, 38. To save the rule and the bill from defeat by making the last minute changes necessary, the special rule (House Resolution 495) provided for consideration of a motion by the majority leader to concur in the Senate amendment with an amendment printed in Part A of the Rules Committee report, "modified by the amendment printed in Part B"—the latter amendment being the game changer.

8. Ian Swanson and Scott Wong, "Ryan: Budget Process 'Stinks,'" *The Hill*, October 27, 2015.

9. "Anatomy of a Vote," *CQ Weekly*, November 2, 2015, 38.

10. *Congressional Record*, October 29, 2015, H7339.

11. "A Better Way: Our Vision for a Confident America," June 16, 2016, 5, accessed at http://abetterway.speaker.gov/.

12. "A Better Way," 16–17.

13. HR 2029, Military Construction Appropriations, 2016, was used as the base bill for the final omnibus measure.

14. David M. Herszenhorn, "Congress Passes $1.8 Trillion Spending Measure," *New York Times*, December 18, 2015.

15. Don Wolfensberger, "Is There Hope for the House?," *The Hill*, January 11, 2017.

16. *Congressional Record*, January 3, 2017, H5.

17. Bill Heniff Jr., "Congressional Budget Resolutions," Congressional Research Service Report RL30297, November 16, 2015, table 12, "Dates of Final Adoption of the Budget Resolution," 29–30.

18. James V. Saturno and Jessica Tollestrup, "Continuing Resolutions: Overview of Components and Recent Practices," Congressional Research

Service Report R42647, January 14, 2016, table 2, "Number and Duration of Continuing Resolutions (CRs): FY 1998–FY2016," 13.

19. "A Pledge to America: A New Governing Agenda Built on the Priorities of Our Nation, the Principles We Stand For, and America's Founding Values," September 23, 2010, http://pledge.gop.gov/resources/library/documents/pledge/a-pledge-to-america.pdf.

20. *Congressional Record*, January 5, 2011, H5–6.

21. "Rules of the House," House Resolution 5, *Congressional Record*, January 5, 2011, H7–10.

22. "Rules of the House," H19.

23. "Rules of the House," H22.

24. "Rules of the House," H7–10.

25. Under rules adopted at the beginning of each Congress, the majority party has the privilege of claiming the first ten bill numbers (HR 1–HR 10) as placeholders for its priority legislation, even if the actual text is not available until a later date. The minority is allotted the next ten bill numbers (HR 11–HR 20).

26. A special rule is termed "modified open" if it requires amendments to be preprinted in the *Congressional Record* in advance of their consideration and/or it sets a time limit on amendments, either in the aggregate or individually.

27. Survey of amendments to HR 1, 112th Congress, www.congress.gov/bill/112th-congress/house-bill/1/amendments?q={"search":["hr1"]}&r=1&pageSort=asc&pageSize=250.

28. Amendment 404, offered by Mr. Walden, *Congressional Record*, February 17, 2011, H1096; adopted February 17, 2011, 244 to 181, H1140.

29. Democrats switched to structured rules on appropriations bills in 2010 because of a proliferation of amendments being offered by Republicans—mostly aimed at eliminating pork barrel projects. Speaker Ryan switched to structured rules on appropriations bills in 2016, ostensibly to filter out politically motivated Democratic amendments.

30. Steve LaTourette, "Why the House Will Miss John Boehner," *Politico*, September 27, 2015.

31. Frank Oliveri, "Cardinals with Clipped Wings," *CQ Weekly*, October 21, 2013, 1753.

5. Whither the War Power?

1. In a January 16, 1970, memorandum to President Nixon, White House domestic policy aide Daniel Patrick Moynihan wrote, "The time may

have come when the issue of race could benefit from a period of 'benign neglect.' The subject has been too much talked about." Moynihan was urging a cooling of rhetoric and not an abandonment of policies dealing with poverty and problems of the inner cities, but the leaked quotation was taken out of context and dogged him for the rest of this career. For the text of the memo, see *Daniel Patrick Moynihan: A Portrait in Letters of an American Visionary*, ed. Steven R. Weisman (Philadelphia, Penn.: Perseus Books, 2010), 211–15.

2. *James Madison: Writings* (New York: Literary Classics of the United States, 1999), "Letter to Thomas Jefferson, April 2, 1798," 586–87. Madison goes on to caution that "if the opinion of the president, and not the facts and proofs . . . are to sway the judgment of Congress in declaring war," the people will be "cheated out of the best ingredients in their government, the safeguards of peace." Madison's specific concern was over President John Adams's saber-rattling with France and the fear the president would use various means to manipulate Congress into supporting what became known as the quasi-war with France.

3. The two cases arising from the quasi-war with France around the turn of the nineteenth century are *Bas v. Tingy*, 4 US 37 (1800) and *Talbot v. Seeman*, 5 US 1 (1801). For a discussion, see Louis Fisher, *Presidential War Power* (Lawrence, Kans.: University of Kansas Press, 1995), 18–19.

4. Fisher, *Presidential War Power*, 70, 84–91.

5. "US Involvement in the Vietnam War: The Gulf of Tonkin and Escalation, 1964," Office of the Historian, US Department of State, https://history .state.gov/milestones/1961-1968/gulf-of-tonkin.

6. HJ Res. 1145, 88th Congress, "Joint Resolution to Promote the Maintenance of International Peace and Security in Southeast Asia." Congress finally repealed the resolution in 1971 as part of a foreign military sales act, which Nixon signed into law. Public Law 88–408, approved August 10, 1964, https://ourdocuments.gov/doc_large_image .php?doc=98.

7. HJ Res. 542, 93rd Congress, "A Joint Resolution Concerning the War Powers of the Congress and the President, Public Law 93–148," November 7, 1973 (enacted over the veto of President Nixon). Text of resolution at Fisher, *Presidential War Power*, appendix E, "War Powers Resolution of 1973, 214–18" (absent sections 5–7, expedited congressional procedures, which can be found in *House Rules and Manual*, 114th Congress, "Resolutions Privileged for Consideration in the House," sec. 1013.2, War Powers).

8. "Veto of the War Powers Resolution," October 24, 1973, in *Public Papers of the Presidents of the United States: Richard Nixon, 1973*, 311 (Washington, D.C.: US Government Printing Office, 1975), 893–95.

9. Charlie Savage, *Power Wars: Inside Obama's Post-9/11 Presidency* (New York: Little, Brown, 2015), 640. Savage points out that President Jimmy Carter's Office of Legal Counsel in 1980 concluded that the sixty-day time limit on a presidential commitment of troops was a "constitutional limit on presidential power, and no subsequent administration has revoked that memorandum opinion."

10. Charles A. Stevenson, *Congress at War: The Politics of Conflict Since 1789* (Washington, D.C.: Potomac Books, 2007); Richard F. Grimmett, "The War Powers Resolution: After Thirty-Six Years," Congressional Research Service, Washington, D.C., April 22, 2010.

11. Norman J. Ornstein and Thomas E. Mann, "When Congress Checks Out," *Foreign Affairs*, November–December 2006, 67–82.

12. William G. Howell and Jon C. Pevehouse, "When Congress Stops Wars," *Foreign Affairs*, September 1, 2007.

13. *Boston Globe* questionnaire on executive power, December 20, 2007, www.ontheissues.org/Archive/2007_Exec_Power_War_+_Peace.htm.

14. Don Wolfensberger, "Congress' War Dance Is a Salsa Sidestep," *Roll Call*, "Procedural Politics," April 12, 2011.

15. Senate Resolution 85, 112th Congress, 1st Session, *Congressional Record*, March 1, 2011, S1075–76.

16. "Letter from the President Regarding the Commencement of Operations in Libya," H. Doc. 112–14, www.gpo.gov/fdsys/pkg/CDOC-112hdoc14/pdf/CDOC-112hdoc14.pdf.

17. *Congressional Record*, March 28, 2011, S1880–81.

18. Remarks by the President in Address to the Nation on Libya, National Defense University, Washington, D.C., March 28, 2011, https://obamawhitehouse.archives.gov/the-press-office/2011/03/28/remarks-president-address-nation-libya.

19. Savage, *Power Wars*, 639.

20. Savage, 640–45.

21. HR 1540, 112th Congress, National Defense Authorization Act, Fiscal Year 2012. The Conyers amendment was adopted on May 26, 2011, by a vote of 416–5.

22. Kucinich's resolution was only privileged for floor consideration because the special rule made it so, contrary to his claim that it was privileged under the terms of the War Powers Resolution. That would only have been the case if the resolution had been reported from the House Foreign Affairs Committee, which it had not been. It was not the first time, however, that the majority leadership had given him leave to bring up such resolutions as a safety valve to let off pent-up frustrations and allow for debate over administration war policies, whether under Democratic or Republican presidents, and whether in Iraq, Afghanistan, or beyond.

23. H. Res. 294, 112th Congress, providing for consideration of H. Res. 292, regarding deployment of United States Armed Forces in Libya, and providing for consideration of H. Con. Res. 51, Libya War Powers Resolution. Debate on the special rule at *Congressional Record*, June 3, 2011, H3990–98. Adopted, 257–156.

24. *Congressional Record*, June 24, 2011, H4534–64, for debates on the special rule (H. Res. 328—a closed rule allowing no amendments), and on the two measures (HJ Res. 68 and HR 2278).

25. SJ Res. 20, 112th Congress. A joint resolution authorizing the limited use of the support of the United States Armed Forces in support of the NATO mission in Libya, introduced by Senator John Kerry, June 21, 2011; ordered reported by the Senate Foreign Relations Committee, June 28, 2011, by a 14–5 vote (Senate Report 112–27, June 29, 2011). Four committee Republicans voted in favor of reporting, and five, including ranking member Richard Lugar, voted against.

26. *Congressional Record*, July 5, 2011, S4314. Corker was referring not to Obama's May 20 letter, which Representative Foxx had chided, but to the president's thirty-two-page letter to Congress on June 15 (pursuant to a directive in the Boehner resolution) in which he elaborated on the "nonhostilities" exception to the War Powers Act and again expressed support for the draft Kerry-McCain et al. resolution in support of the US mission in Libya.

27. *Congressional Record*, July 5, 2011, S4319.

28. Letter from the President to the Speaker of the House and President of the Senate regarding the War Powers Resolution Report for Libya, September 14, 2012, https://oamawhitehouse.archives.gov/the-press-office/2012/09/14/letter-president.

29. Savage, *Power Wars*, 650.

30. Peter Baker and Jonathan Weisman, "Obama Seeks Approval by Congress for Strike in Syria," *New York Times*, August 31, 2013.

31. Adam Entous, Janet Hook, and Carol E. Lee, "Inside White House, a Head-Spinning Reversal on Chemical Weapons," *Wall Street Journal*, September 16, 2013, cited by Savage, *Power Wars*, 653–54.

32. "Iraq and Syria Policy: Cash and Wary," *CQ Almanac, 2014* (Washington, D.C.: CQ Roll Call, 2015), 5–9.

33. "Statement by the President on ISIL," September 10, 2014, https://obama whitehouse.archives.gov/the-press-office/2014/09/10/statement-president-isil-1.

34. "Letter from the President to the Speaker of the House—War Powers Resolution Regarding Iraq," September 23, 2014, https://obamawitehouse.archives.gov/the-press-office/2014/09/23/letter-president-war-powers-resolution-regafrding-iraq.

35. "Iraq and Syria Policy," 5–9.

36. Spencer Ackerman, "White House Says Expired War Powers Timetable Irrelevant to ISIS Campaign," *The Guardian*, October 6, 2014.

37. See Donald R. Wolfensberger, "Congress and Policymaking in an Age of Terrorism," in *Congress Reconsidered*, 8th edition, ed. Lawrence C. Dodd and Bruce I. Oppenheimer (Washington, D.C.: CQ Press, 2005), 346–47; and Bruce Ackerman, "The War Against ISIS Is Unconstitutional," *Lawfare*, War Powers Blog, May 5, 2016, www.lawfareblog.com /war-against-isis-unconstitutional.

38. "Letter from the President to the Congress: Authorization for the Use of United States Armed Forces in Connection with the Islamic State of Iraq and the Levant, February 11, 2015," https://obamawhitehouse.archives.gov /sites/default/files/docs/aumf_021115.pdf.

39. Jim Acosta and Jeremy Diamond, "Obama ISIS Fight Request Sent to Congress," CNN, February 12, 2015, www.cnn.com/2015/02/11/politics/isis -aumf-white-house-congress/.

40. Acosta and Diamond, "Obama ISIS Fight Request Sent to Congress."

41. Center for National Security Studies, "Congressional Hearings on an ISIL AUMF," http://cnss.client.fatbeehive.com/pages/congressional-hearings -on-an-isil-aumf.html.

42. S. 1587, 114th Congress, "Authority for the Use of Military Force Against the Islamic State of Iraq and the Levant Act, Introduced by Sen. Tim Kaine (for himself and Mr. Flake)," June 16, 2015, available at www .congress.gov.

43. Scott Wong, "GOP: Obama War Request Is Dead," *The Hill*, April 13, 2015, http://thehill.com/policy/defense/238619-gop-obama-war-request-is -dead.

44. Russell Berman, "The War Against ISIS Will Go Undeclared," *The Atlantic*, April 15, 2015, www.theatlantic.com/politics/archive/2015/04/the-war -against-isis-will-go-undeclared/390618.

45. Jordain Carney, "Obama's Move in Syria Reignites War Powers Debate," *The Hill*, October 30, 2015, http://thehill.com/blogs/floor-action /senate/258726-syria-troop-deployment-stirs-war-bill-debate.

46. "President Obama Addresses the Nation on Keeping the American People Safe," December 6, 2015, https://medium.com/@ObamaWhiteHouse /president-obama-addresses-the-nation-on-keeping-the-american-people-safe -b4cfa8a0f143#.eao9hx8w0.

47. SJ Res. 29, 114th Congress, "Authorization for Use of Military Force Against the Islamic State of Iraq and the Levant and Its Associated Forces," January 20, 2016, available at www.congress.gov. Other members introducing AUMFs in the 113th and/or 114th Congresses include Senator Robert

Menendez (D-NJ), Representative Frank Wolf (R-VA), Representative John Larson (D-CT), Representative Scott Rigell (R-VA), and Representative Adam Schiff (D-CA).

48. SA 4496, Kaine (for himself, Mr. Flake, and Mr. Nelson), and SA 4497, Mr. Kaine (for himself, and Mr. Merkley), *Congressional Record*, June 7, 2016, S3563–65.

49. "Letter from the President to Congress, 'Supplemental 6-Month War Powers Letter,'" December 5, 2016, https://obamawhitehouse.archives. gov/the-press-office/2016/12/05/letter-president-supplemental-6-month-war -powers-letter.

50. "Report on the Legal and Policy Frameworks Guiding the United States' Use of Military Force and Related National Security Operations," December 2016, https://obamawhitehouse.archives.gov/sites/whitehouse.gov /files/documents/Legal_Policy_Report.pdf.

51. "Fact Sheet: Presidential Memorandum—Legal and Policy Transparency Concerning United States' Use of Military Force and Related National Security Operations," https://obamawhitehouse.archives.gov/the-press-office/2016/12/05 /fact-sheet-presidential-memorandum-legal-and-policy-transparency.

52. "Hoyer Statement on White House Report on Use of Military Force," press release, December 5, 2016, available at www.democraticwhip.gov.

53. Rebecca Kheel, "White House Report Details Obama's Military Force Rules," *The Hill*, December 5, 2016, http://thehill.com/policy/defense/308832 -white-house-releases-report-on-obamas-military-force-rules.

54. Josh Lederman, "Obama Legacy: Handing Trump a Broad View of War Powers," *AP*, December 5, 2016, http://bigstory.ap.org/article/4b970 9c55c5a4d10ac499e16b151ade9/us-wars-grounded-law-white-house-says; Seth McLaughlin, "Obama Evades Congress, Stretches War Powers in Precedent for Trump," *Washington Times*, December 25, 2016.

6. Congress and the Iran Nuclear Deal: Rational Reactor or Design Flaw?

1. Robert Litwak, *Iran's Nuclear Chess: After the Deal* (Washington, D.C.: Woodrow Wilson International Center for Scholars, 2015), 8.

2. Litwak, *Iran's Nuclear Chess*, 8.

3. Arms Control Association, "Timeline of Nuclear Diplomacy with Iran," August 1, 2016, https://armscontrol.org/print/5654.

4. Executive agreements must have some grounding in authority previously granted by Congress (or by the Constitution); in this instance, the

president could point to the sanctions waiver authority Congress had given him in various sanctions acts.

5. This is paraphrasing the constitutional scholar Edward Corwin's famous line that the Constitution is an invitation for the president and Congress to struggle for the privilege of directing foreign policy. See, for example, Lee Hamilton, *A Creative Tension: The Foreign Policy Roles of the President and Congress* (Washington, D.C. and Baltimore, Md.: Woodrow Wilson Center Press and Johns Hopkins University Press, 2002), 5–6.

6. HR 2194, 111th Congress, "The Comprehensive Iran Sanctions, Accountability and Divestment Act of 2010, Introduced by Rep. Howard Berman, April 30, 2009; Public Law 111–195 (July 1, 2010)." President Obama allowed the extension of the act in 2016 to become law without his signature because he feared it might interfere with the Iran Nuclear Agreement.

7. *Congressional Record*, July 23, 2014, S4767.

8. S. 615, 114th Congress, "The Iran Nuclear Agreement Review Act, Introduced by Senator Bob Corker," February 27, 2015.

9. Jesse Byrnes, "Obama Threatens to Veto Iran Bill," *The Hill*, February 28, 2015, http://thehill.com/blog-briefing-room/234223-obama-theatens-to-veto-iran-bill.

10. *Congressional Record*, March 3, 2015, H1528–31.

11. Peter Baker, "GOP Senators' Letter to Iran About Nuclear Deal Angers White House," *New York Times*, March 9, 2015, www.nytimes.com/2015/03/10/world/asia/white-house-faults-gop-senators-letter-to-irans-leaders.html.

12. Senator Tom Cotton, "Open Letter to the Leaders of the Islamic Republic of Iran," March 9, 2015, www.cotton.senate.gov/?p=press_release&id=120; Don Wolfensberger, "Cotton Balls-Up Diplomatic Protocol with Letter," Procedural Politics (column), *Roll Call*, March 16, 2015.

13. Arms Control Association, "Timeline," 18.

14. Jonathan Weisman and Peter Baker, "Obama Yields, Allowing Congress Say on Iran Nuclear Deal," *New York Times*, April 14, 2015.

15. Cosponsors: S. 615—114th Congress, Sponsor: Senator Corker, Ob (R-TN), 66 current, includes 11 original, available at www.congress.gov.

16. S. 615, 114th Congress, "The Iran Nuclear Agreement Act of 2015, Reported by Mr. Corker, with an Amendment, April 14, 2015." No report was filed on the bill.

17. The *House Rules and Manual* (sec. 1130, 113th Cong.) includes a 170-page section titled "Statutory Legislative Procedures," which includes more than fifty provisions of law under thirty-three categories providing for expedited consideration of everything from executive reorganization,

war powers, and budget impoundment control to trade, arms control, land policy, and nuclear waste policy.

18. *Congressional Record*, April 23, 2015, S2386. Kaine mistakenly said September 27, but it was clear that he meant February 27, the actual date the bill was introduced.

19. *Congressional Record*, April 23, 2015, S2387.

20. *Congressional Record*, S2361.

21. HR 1191, 114th Congress, "Protecting Volunteer Firefighters and Emergency Responders Act, Introduced by Mr. Barletta," March 2, 2016, available at www.congress.gov.

22. *Congressional Record*, April 23, 2015, Senate Amendment 1140, S2381.

23. Don Wolfensberger, "Why the Senate Plays Legislative Bait-and-Switch," Procedural Politics (column), *Roll Call*, June 15, 2015. The column also notes that the same bait-and-switch process was used in May 2015 to tack a Senate-reported Trade Promotion Authority bill's language onto an unrelated House bill, giving organizations a right to appeal denial of their tax-exempt-status applications. Trade Promotion Authority, previously known as "fast-track trade negotiating authority," authorizes the president to negotiate trade agreements and have them considered by Congress under expedited procedures. It was renewed for six years in 2015, although President Trump has since withdrawn from the Trans-Pacific Partnership trade agreement.

24. Wolfensberger, "Why the Senate Plays Legislative Bait-and-Switch."

25. *Congressional Record*, April 23, 2015, S2385.

26. HR 1191, 114th Congress, Amendments, at www.congress.gov.

27. *CQ Almanac, 2015* (Washington, D.C.: CQ Roll Call, 2016), 114th Congress, First Session, vote nos. 167 and 168, S28.

28. HR 1191, 114th Congress, "All Actions," available at www.congress.gov.

29. HR 1191, Public Law 114–17.

30. *Congressional Record*, September 8, 2015, S6441.

31. *Congressional Record*, HJ Res. 61, 114th Congress, S6438–41.

32. HJ Res. 64, 114th Congress, introduced by Mr. Royce, August 4, 2015, disapproving of the agreement transmitted by the president on July 19, 2015, relating to the nuclear program of Iran; and, H. Res. 408, 114th Congress, introduced by Mr. Sessions, providing for the consideration of the joint resolution (HJ Res. 64), disapproving of the agreement transmitted by the president on July 19, 2015, relating to the nuclear program of Iran, reported by the House Committee on Rules, September 8, 2015; laid on the table September 17, 2015.

33. Don Wolfensberger, "Iran Review Moves Recall 'Duck-and-Cover' Days," Procedural Politics (column), *Roll Call*, September 30, 2015.

34. Legislative summaries and actions on the various measures are from Congress's website, www.congress.gov.

7. Governing in a Political World

1. Woodrow Wilson, *Congressional Government: A Study in American Politics* (Baltimore, Md.: Johns Hopkins University Press, 1956; originally published in 1885), 197.

2. Wilson, *Congressional Government*, 87.

3. Jenna Johnson, "Trump's Grand Promises to 'Very, Very Quickly' Replace Obamacare Run Into Reality," *Washington Post*, July 18, 2017.

4. "S. Con. Res. 3, 115th Congress, a Concurrent Resolution Setting Forth the Congressional Budget for the United States Government for Fiscal Year 2017, . . . Adopted by the House and Senate on Jan. 13, 2017," www .congress.gov/bill/115th-congress/senate-concurrent-resolution/3?q=%7B% 22search%22%3A%5B%22sconres3%22%5D%7D&r=1.

5. See, for example, Congressional Budget Office, "Cost Estimate, HR 1628, Obamacare Repeal Reconciliation as of 2017," July 18, 2017, www .cbo.gov/publication/52939.

6. Henry C. Jackson, "6 Promises Trump Had Made About Health Care," *Politico*, March 13, 2017, www.politico.com/story/2017/03/trump -obamacare-promises-236021.

7. "H. Res. 228, 115th Congress, a Resolution Providing for Consideration of the Bill (HR 1628) Providing for Reconciliation Pursuant to Title II of the Concurrent Resolution on the Budget for Fiscal Year 2017," http:rules .house.gov.

8. *Congressional Record*, March 24, 2017, H2441, available at www .congress.gov.

9. Dan Merica and Lauren Fox, "Trump Calls GOP Health Care Bill 'Mean' and Democrats Pounce, Republicans Worry," CNN Politics, June 20, 2017, www.cnn.com/2017/06/20/politics/trump-mean-health-care/.

10. Sean Sullivan, Juliet Eilperin, and Kelsey Snell, "GOP Defections Spell Trouble for Health Care Bill," *Washington Post*, September 23, 2017.

11. Peter Sullivan, "GOP Chairman Declares Bipartisan Obam-acare Fix Dead," *The Hill*, September 19, 2017, http://thehill.com /policy/healthcare/351431-gop-chairman-declares-bipartisan-obamacare-fix-dead.

12. Juliet Eilperin, Sean Sullivan, and Amy Goldstein, "Lacking Support, GOP Drops Its Health Care Bill," *Washington Post*, September 27, 2017.

13. Sullivan, Eilperin, and Snell, "GOP Defections."

14. Wilson, *Congressional Government*, 198.

15. Wilson, 199.

16. Wilson would switch horses in his subsequent work, thanks in large part to the example of Theodore Roosevelt's vigorous presidency. Now the president was informer-in-chief, shaping public opinion as leader of his party, the nation, and, by the power of persuasion, the Congress. The most noted line from this work is: "The president is at liberty, both in law and conscience, to be as big a man as he can be." Woodrow Wilson, *Constitutional Government in the United States* (New York: Columbia University Press, 1908), 70.

17. Wilson, *Congressional Government*, 199.

18. Commission on Political Reform, Bipartisan Policy Center, "Governing in a Polarized America: A Bipartisan Blueprint to Strengthen Our Democracy," https://bipartisanpolicy.org/library/governing-polarized-america-bipartisan-blueprint-strengthen-our-democracy/.

19. Wilson, *Congressional Government*, 200.

Glossary

The following definitions are drawn from "Glossary of Congressional Terms," in *Congressional Quarterly's Guide to Congress*, 2nd ed. (Washington, D.C.: Congressional Quarterly, 1976), xxiii–xxxi; and Walter J. Oleszek, *Congressional Procedures and the Policy Process*, 7th ed. (Washington, D.C.: CQ Press, 2007), 329–41.

APPROPRIATIONS BILL: Legislation that provides the actual monies to fund an authorized program or agency. Twelve regular appropriations bills are supposed to be enacted by the beginning of a fiscal year (October 1). In recent years, these have been few and seldom, necessitating a continuing appropriations resolution and eventually one or more omnibus appropriations bills that combine two or more of the regular appropriations measures.

AUTHORIZATION BILL: Legislation that establishes or continues an agency or program either on a permanent basis, or for a specified period, and establishes the goals, purposes, activities, and, sometimes, an overall spending ceiling for the program or agency. Authorizations are supposed to be enacted before money is appropriated for them, although it is not unusual for the reverse sequence to occur, or for unauthorized entities to be appropriated.

AUMF (AUTHORIZATIONS FOR THE USE OF MILITARY FORCE): An authorization by law, enacted by Congress, for the use of military force by the president. It has been used in modern times in lieu of a declaration of war.

BLUE-SLIP RESOLUTION: A simple resolution by the House of Representatives, printed on blue paper, that, if adopted, is attached to a Senate bill and returned to the Senate without further consideration of the bill. The blue-slip resolution asserts that the Senate bill violates one of the constitutional prerogatives of the House. It is frequently used on Senate bills that violate the Constitution's "origination clause," which requires that all revenue bills (and, by precedent, appropriations bills) must originate in the House. (In the Senate, by contrast, "blue-slipping" is the paper used by senators to offer their opinions on executive or judicial nominees from their home states.)

BUDGET: The document, required by law to be sent to Congress by the president by the first Monday in February, containing estimated revenues and expenditures for next fiscal year and requests for specific appropriations amounts for all government departments and agencies.

BUDGET RECONCILIATION: A process that allows for the Budget Committee to include in the annual congressional budget resolution instructions to committees to report legislation containing provisions that achieve specified reductions in the deficit.

BUDGET RESOLUTION: A concurrent resolution of the House and Senate required by the 1974 Budget Act to be adopted by April 15 for the fiscal year beginning on October 1. The resolution contains overall levels for spending, revenues, the deficit, and the debt. The final resolution provides allocations of spending authority to committees and may contain reconciliation instructions.

BYRD RULE: A Senate rule in the Budget Act (named after Senator Robert Byrd) that prohibits the inclusion of "extraneous matter" in budget reconciliation legislation that either is not budgetary in nature (pertaining to outlays or revenues) or that increases the deficit beyond the ten-year time frame. If a point of order is sustained in the Senate against a provision, the provision is automatically dropped from the bill. A point of order can only be waived by a three-fifths vote.

CHAIRMAN'S MARK: The draft legislation put before a committee by its chairperson for the purpose of entertaining further amendments before the measure is reported to the House or Senate.

CLOSED RULE: A special rule (a simple resolution by the House of Representatives) reported by the House Rules Committee that prohibits amendments to the legislation made in order for House consideration by the rule.

Glossary

CLOTURE: The process by which a filibuster (extended debate) can be terminated in the Senate. It begins with the filing of a motion signed by sixteen senators to end debate on a specified motion or measure. It can be considered by the Senate on the second day after it is filed. A sixty-vote majority is required to invoke cloture. To invoke cloture against a change in Senate rules requires a two-thirds vote.

COMMITTEE OF THE WHOLE: The committee of the House of Representatives—formally known as the Committee of the Whole House on the State of the Union—that comprises the entire House membership. It is used only for considering authorization, appropriations, or revenue measures, and primarily for considering amendments to legislation. It has a smaller quorum requirement of 100 members of Congress (instead of 218) and allows for fewer procedural motions (for example, the previous question motion). Amendments adopted in the Committee of the Whole must be readopted in the House of Representatives after it rises. The Senate does not have a Committee of the Whole.

COMPANION BILL: A bill introduced in one body that is identical or similar to a bill introduced in the other body, usually by design, to facilitate the two houses proceeding along parallel lines. If the companion bills are introduced at the behest of the administration, they sometimes carry the designation "(by request)" after the sponsor's name.

CONFERENCE REPORT: A report of a House–Senate conference committee appointed to resolve differences between the two bodies on a measure both chambers have passed. The conference report includes the compromise legislative language as well as a "joint explanatory statement of the managers" from the House and Senate explaining how each of the differences were dealt with by the conference committee. A conference report must be signed by a majority of the conferees from each house (no vote is required). Not all bills differing between the houses are sent to conference; some are resolved by exchanging amendments between the houses until a final agreement is reached on the same language.

DISAPPEARING QUORUM: A tactic used by the minority to block action on a pending matter by members not responding to their names when called by the clerk for purposes of determining a quorum, either on a substantive vote or a quorum call. The practice was abolished by the speaker of the House of Representatives, Tom Reed, in 1889 by having the clerk take down names of members he saw in the chamber who had not registered their presence.

DISAPPROVAL RESOLUTIONS: Usually, joint resolutions authorized by a law to enable Congress to reject a recommendation formally presented by the president. They are usually considered under expedited procedures,

167

ensuring that they are presented to the president if passed by both houses. If the president vetoes a disapproval resolution, it is returned to Congress, where a two-thirds vote is required to override the veto and block the president's proposal.

ENTITLEMENTS: These are often referred to as mandatory spending, or those benefits authorized in permanent law that are dispersed to qualifying individuals according to the terms of the law—Social Security and Medicare being two of the biggest and most prominent entitlements. They are in contrast to discretionary spending, which is determined by Congress each year in appropriations bills.

EXPEDITED PROCEDURES: These are sometimes referred to as "fast-track legislation," used in some laws to facilitate consideration by Congress of certain matters presented to it by the president. They can apply to either joint resolutions of approval or disapproval. They provide specified time limits by which a committee must report the resolution or it is discharged, and specified time limits both for debating and taking final action on the joint resolution—thereby precluding a filibuster.

FILIBUSTER: A delaying tactic in the Senate that relies on senators holding the floor for an extended period of debate, thereby blocking final action on the pending measure (or nomination). Since 1970, there have been fewer actual filibusters with the institution of a "two-track" system, whereby the filibuster is set aside (without jeopardizing the right of the filibustering senator) and other legislation is considered. The filibuster can be ended if sixty senators vote to invoke cloture.

FISCAL YEAR: This is the twelve-month federal budget year that begins on October 1 and ends on September 30.

FIVE-MINUTE RULE: The rule in the House of Representatives that limits members to five minutes to speak on an amendment in the Committee of the Whole after general debate is concluded. It is more customary today to consider amendments under structured rules from the Rules Committee that specify how much debate time is allowed for amendments made in order by the rule. Only an open rule allows any member to speak for five minutes on a pending amendment.

FLOOR MANAGER: The senator or representative who manages a particular piece of legislation on the Senate or House floor. It is usually the chairperson of the committee or subcommittee to which the legislation was initially referred. The managers both apportion time to others for debate and represent the committee in either supporting or opposing amendments that are offered. In the Senate, the majority leader often acts as floor manager because he or she always has the first right of recognition to offer motions or amendments.

GENERAL DEBATE: The debate time for a bill considered in the COMMITTEE OF THE WHOLE before amendments are considered under the five-minute rule. If a bill is privileged for consideration in the Committee of the Whole, general debate time is set by a unanimous consent request. Most bills are brought under a special rule that allocates general debate time (often just one hour), equally divided between the chairperson and ranking minority members of the committee(s) that reported the bill.

GERMANENESS: The House rule prohibits amendments to legislation that do not pertain to the subject matter of the measure. The Senate germaneness rule, by contrast, applies only to general appropriations bills and to amendments offered to bills after CLOTURE has been invoked.

JOINT COMPREHENSIVE PLAN OF ACTION: This was a stage in the Iran nuclear negotiations paving the way for a final agreement with the P5+1— the five permanent members of the UN Security Council plus Germany.

MANAGER'S AMENDMENT: An amendment offered by the manager of a bill being considered on the floor, usually given priority consideration by a special rule or unanimous consent before other amendments are offered to the bill. The amendment may be a series of technical changes in the bill or more substantive policy changes to enhance the bill's passage.

MARK UP: The process used in a committee for amending legislation. The bill is read section by section for amendment, and it is marked up to include any amendments that have been adopted.

OPEN RULE: A special rule from the Rules Committee in the House of Representatives that allows for any member to offer any germane amendment during consideration of the bill for amendment under the five-minute rule in the Committee of the Whole.

POINT OF ORDER: An objection raised in committee or from the floor to a perceived violation of a standing rule of the House or Senate. If the presiding officer sustains the point of order, the offending act is mitigated. If the point of order is overruled, the person bringing it can appeal the ruling of the chair. The chair's ruling can be overturned by majority vote.

PREVIOUS QUESTION: A motion used during consideration of a measure in the House of Representatives (but not in the committee of the whole) to determine whether the House is prepared to bring the matter to a final vote. It is used most on special rules and simple House resolutions after the hour of debate expires. If adopted, the House proceeds to vote on the resolution. If rejected, someone who opposed the previous question (usually the minority party manager) is recognized for an hour and may offer a germane amendment (or amendments) to the pending measure.

PROCEDURAL RULE: Either a standing rule of the House or Senate that specifies what procedures shall be used in what situations, either in a committee or on the floor, or a special rule from the Rules Committee or by unanimous consent that provides for some new procedure to be followed or that waives a standing rule.

RIDERS: Legislative provisions attached to appropriations bills by the appropriations committees in violation of the standing rules of the House and Senate. In the House, they are usually protected against points of order by waivers in the special rule for considering the bill, although they may be exposed to a point of order if an authorizing chairman objects to their inclusion.

SELF-EXECUTING RULE: A special rule from the House Rules Committee that provides for the automatic adoption of an amendment (or amendments) contained in the Rules Committee's report on the rule. The self-executed amendments are considered adopted to the bill being made in order upon the adoption of the special rule. The process obviates the need for debate or a vote on the amendments when the bill is called up for consideration.

SEQUESTRATION: A process established in the Budget Act (and subsequent budget agreements) that provides for across the board cuts in domestic and defense discretionary spending if Congress does not meet its deficit target or exceeds a statutory spending ceiling.

SPECIAL RULES: Simple House resolutions (also known as rules or order of business resolutions) reported by the House Rules Committee that provide for the consideration of legislation from other committees (whether reported or not). Their main functions are to give privileged consideration status to the bill, regardless of its position on the Union Calendar (to which all bills that directly or indirectly appropriate money or raise revenues are placed according to the date reported to the House from committee); provide for general debate time; establish an amendment process (or not); and waive any standing rules that may otherwise inhibit consideration of the bill. The rules may be open, structured, or closed to amendments.

STRUCTURED RULE: A special rule resolution from the House Rules Committee that allows for consideration only of amendments printed (or referenced) in the Rules Committee report on the rule. Members are notified in advance of the Rules Committee meeting that a structured rule is being contemplated and are given a deadline before the meeting to file their amendments with the committee.

SUBSTITUTE AMENDMENT: An amendment offered to replace a section or provision in a bill. It is different from an amendment in the nature of a substitute that replaces the entire text of the bill.

Index

Page numbers in italics refer to figures or tables

171

Congress: evolving process and
procedures of, 7; executive
agreements and, 107, 160*n*4;
final report on Obama doctrine
in 2016 to, 102–3; First
Congress, 11–13; fiscal cliffs
of, 69–70; fiscal control by,
68; health care effort of 103rd
Congress and, 41, 42; legislating
versus governing, 124–27,
136–39; Libya and, 84–93;
power plays of, 5; press and,
139; revolts in 2006, 2010 and
2015, 6; self-executing rules
of, *143*; voting in, 126–27. *See
also* House of Representatives;
Senate
Congressional Accountability Act of
1995, 29, 150*n*10
Congressional Budget and
Impoundment Control Act of
1974 (Budget Act), 68, 69, 129
Congressional Budget Office, 52, 130
congressional committees:
partisanship and amendments in,
126. *See also* House committees
congressional governing: big
picture governing, 135–39;
Commission on Political Reform
on improving, 138; informing
function of, 136, 137, 139;
legislating versus governing,
124–27, 136–39; Wilson on,
125, 126, 136–39. *See also*
governing
Congressional Government
(Wilson), 125, 126
congressional leadership: as
intricate balancing act, 76.
See also majority leadership;

minority leaders; Senate majority
leader; speakers of the House
congressional procedures. *See*
procedures
congressional rules: expedited
procedures, 111–12, 161*n*17;
framers of Constitution on,
9–10; as neutral as early
Congress evolved, 11. *See also*
House rules; procedures; *specific
topics*
Conrad, Kent, 49–52
Constitution: framers of Constitution,
9–10, 13; origination clause,
114; parliamentary system versus
American constitutional system,
136
Contract with America, 2, 26, 27
Conyers, John, 89–90, 157*n*21
Corker, Bob, 92, 108–9, 111–16,
121, 158*n*26
Cotton, Tom, 110, 116
culture of campaigning, of
Congress: culture of legislating
replaced by, 6–7, 125; war
powers of Congress and, 78
culture of legislating, of Congress,
6–7, 125
cut-as-you-go (CUTGO) budgeting
rules, 71

Dalzell, John, 35
debate: attempts to limit in 19th
century, 16; general debate,
18, 47, 169; lack of seriousness
about, 126
debt limit, Boehner and, 62, 63
defense authorization bill,
amendments about Libya to
2011, 90, 157*nn*21–22, 158*n*23

Democratic Congress, Obamacare
and, 38
Democratic resistance: to
Obamacare repeal and replace
attempts, 130; to Trump, 135
Democrats. *See* Blue Dog
Democrats; House Democrats;
Senate Democrats
Democrats, procedural tools of:
Obamacare and, 49, 50, 53–55.
See also House Democrats,
procedural shortcuts and
abuses of
dilatory motions, 17, 19, 20
Dingell, John, 25, 149*n*1; health care
legislation and, 39, 40, 152*n*2;
Obamacare and, 43, 48–49
disappearing quorum, 18, 19,
148*n*21, 167
disapproval resolutions, 117, 118,
167–68
Dodd, Chris, 46
Dreier, David, 1, 2, 29, 30, 153*n*21
Dyer, Jim, 75

Elving, Ron, 3–4
entitlements, 168
executive agreements: Congress
and, 107, 160*n*4; of presidents,
104; Senate and, 104. *See also*
Iran nuclear agreement
expedited procedures, 111–12,
161*n*17, 168

factions: Madison on, 10–11, 13;
mitigation of dangers of, 10–11.
See also parties, political
fair play, House rules and, 8
fast-track procedures or legislation.
See expedited procedures

Federalist Papers, The, 9–11
filibuster, 168
First Congress: parliamentary
rules and, 11–12; rules of Select
Committee on Rules, 12–13
fiscal cliffs, of Congress, 69–70
fiscal contortions, of 114th
Congress, 68
fiscal control, by Congress, 68
fiscal year, 168
Fitzgerald, John, 33–34
five-minute rule, 168
Flake, Jeff, 100, 101
floor manager, 168
foreign policy, Congress and:
foreign policy of Obama
and, 104–5; foreign policy of
president and, 104, 161*n*5. *See
also* war powers, of Congress
foreign policy, of Obama: Congress
and, 104–5; Iran nuclear
diplomacy, 107. *See also* Iran
nuclear agreement, Obama and;
war powers, of Obama
foreign policy, of president:
Congress and, 104, 161*n*5;
Senate and, 104. *See also* war
powers, of president
foreign policy, Senate and: foreign
policy of president and, 104. *See
also* foreign policy, Congress and
founders, 8; on rulemaking
responsibility, 9; on war powers
of Congress, 78, 156*n*2
framers of Constitution: on
congressional rules and
procedures, 9–10; emergence of
political parties and, 13
France, quasi-war with, 78,
156*nn*2–3

Index

Slaughter Solution, 53–54
Solomon, Jerry, 2
speaker's committee, 23–24, 36–37
speakers of the House: Freedom
Caucus resolution about, 5; as
head of House Rules Committee,
23; rulings of, 9. *See also specific
topics*
special orders, 18
special rules, 18, 170;
appropriations bill of 2015
and, 63–64, 154*n*7; for
House legislation, *142*; House
unreported measures and, *146*;
modified open special rules, 73,
155*n*26; Obamacare repeal and
replace attempts and, 131, 132;
Reed and, 20, 21, 22. *See also
specific topics*
spending, Budget Act and out-of-
control, 68
Spratt, John, 52
standing rules, 22
structured rules, 170; amendments
to, *145*
Stupak, Bart, 48–49
substitute amendment, 170
Syria, 93–97, 99, 101, 102

Tea Party Republicans, 4, 58,
60–61, 70, 74. *See also* Freedom
Caucus
Truman, Harry, 78, 79
Trump, Donald: budget and, 67;
Democratic resistance to, 135;
Obamacare repeal and replace
attempts and, 128, 130–33
Trumpcare: Obamacare versus,
128–35; Trump's broken promises
about, 130. *See also* Obamacare,
repeal and replace attempts

UN. *See* United Nations
Underwood, Oscar, 35–36
United Nations (UN): Korean
War and, 78–79; Libya and,
84, 86; P5+1 and Iran nuclear
agreement, 105–8, 110, 116

Van Hollen, Chris, 71
Vietnam War, 79–80, 156*n*6

war, quasi-war with France, 78,
156*nn*2–3
war powers, of Congress: AUMFs
and, 78, 82, 83, 95, 98–102,
159*n*47; benign ambivalence
about, 77–78, 82–83; culture of
campaigning and, 78; founders
on, 78, 156*n*2; ISIS and, 95–102;
Korean War and, 78, 79; Libya
and, 86, 88–93; Syria and, 94–
95; Vietnam War and, 79, 80,
156*n*6; war powers of Obama
and, 82, 83, 85, 86, 88–102;
war powers of president and, 77,
78, 121; War Powers Resolution
and, 80–82, 86, 89–90, 92, 93,
98, 157*n*9, 157*n*22, 158*n*23,
158*n*26; World War II and, 78
war powers, of Obama: AUMFs
and, 83, 95, 97, 98–102; final
report on Obama doctrine in
2016 to Congress, 102–3; House
and, 86, 89–91, 99–100; ISIS
and, 95–102; Libya and, 84–93;
Obama on limits of, 83, 84;
Senate and, 87, 91–92, 158*n*26;
Syria and, 93–95; war powers
of Congress and, 82, 83, 85, 86,
88–102; War Powers Resolution
and, 86, 89, 92, 93, 95, 98,
158*n*26

182